RESET
RESET
RESET

DEBRA FILETA
M.A., LPC

HARVEST HOUSE PUBLISHERS
EUGENE. OREGON

For bulk, special sales, or ministry purchases, please call 1-800-547-8979.
Email: Customerservice@hhpbooks.com

Cover design by Faceout Studio, Amanda Hudson

Interior design by KUHN Design Group

M This logo is a federally registered trademark of the Hawkins Children's LLC. Harvest House Publishers, Inc., is the exclusive licensee of this trademark

Reset
Copyright © 2023 by Debra Fileta
Published by Harvest House Publishers
Eugene, Oregon 97408
www.harvesthousepublishers.com

ISBN 978-0-7369-8651-9 (pbk.)
ISBN 978-0-7369-8652-6 (eBook)

Library of Congress Control Number: 2022938676

Printed in the United States of America

23 24 25 26 27 28 29 30 31 / BP / 10 9 8 7 6 5 4 3 2 1

*This book is dedicated to my best friend, forever partner,
and legit number one fan: my husband, John.*

*Thank you for so steadily walking this journey with me, in sync,
step-by-step, and side-by-side. Being married to this therapist
is no small feat, but you've embraced it like no one else could!*

*What a beautiful 15 years it has been,
and here's to many, many more.*

I love you, always and forever.

CONTENTS

FOREWORD

BY CHRISTINE CAINE

I t is not often that you meet someone and click from the first moment, but that is exactly what happened when I met Debra. Yes, we are both fiery Mediterranean women with a passion for Jesus and human flourishing, but it was Debra's wisdom, insight, compassion, humor, transparency, and humility that sealed it for me. You too will discover this for yourself within the pages of this powerful book.

When I became a follower of Jesus, I was desperate to live a life that was pleasing to God and to fulfill my purpose on this earth, all for God's glory. But as well intentioned as I was—and believe me, I was as sincere as I knew how to be—I kept cycling in and out of seasons of defeat. No matter how hard I tried—and believe me, I tried—I could not seem to stop. Having been left in a hospital unnamed and unwanted when I was born, a victim of childhood sexual abuse, marginalized because of my ethnicity and gender, I brought a lot of baggage into my relationship with Jesus and with everyone else.

No matter how hard I prayed, or how often I fasted, or how frequently I went to church or read the Bible, I could not seem to find freedom or healing. I could not break my patterns of destructive behavior. I had no idea that I had the power to control my thoughts and not yield to the demands of my feelings. I was left thinking that I would be stuck in these patterns forever.

Finally, I got desperate enough to talk to a spiritual director who told me that the reason I did not seem to be making progress was because I was trying to modify my behavior from the outside in, rather than from the inside out. She explained to me that with the help of the Holy Spirit living in me, my history did not have to define my destiny. I could reset the trajectory of my life. That conversation changed everything for me and started me on a journey to health—body, soul, and spirit—that has lasted for 35 years so far.

In Matthew 22:37-39, Jesus said, "Love the Lord your God with all your heart, with all your soul, and with all your mind. This is the greatest and most important command. The second is like it: Love your neighbor as yourself" (HCSB). Did you notice that we are to love God from the inside out? Jesus focused on our hearts, our souls, and our minds, because that is where true transformation happens. We can try to modify our behavior, but it usually will not last because nothing has changed in our hearts, souls, and minds, which are the control centers of our lives. If our hearts are broken, our souls wounded, and our minds tormented, we will not fulfill the greatest and most important commandment. Moreover, we will end up loving our neighbors just like we love ourselves, and by that I mean not very well. Can you see how vital it is that we understand the importance of having a constant reset?

I wish I had the book you are holding in your hands now back then. I cannot stress enough the importance of the 31 practices that Debra has unpacked for us. I found myself *Amen*-ing aloud every time Debra introduced us to a new habit with a short lesson and a practical activity, because after all these decades of following Jesus, I truly believe that the only difference between those who walk in the freedom and wholeness that Jesus has made available for us, and those who do not, is our willingness to actually practice these practices. Daily. There are no shortcuts, no quick-fix solutions, and I am grateful for a therapist who has not overpromised and underdelivered. Debra equips and empowers us to go deeper in order to truly change patterns, break habits, and find healing and wholeness. Enjoy the journey, and keep practicing until the practice forms a new you.

With love,
Christine Caine
Founder, A21 and Propel Women

START HERE

IT'S TIME FOR A RESET

There's probably something in your life you want to change. You wouldn't be here if there wasn't. The very fact that a person like you would pick up a book like this tells me, whether small or significant, there's an area of your life where you want to see growth, or healing, or perspective, or motivation. Some sort of progress. Some sort of change. Stop for a moment and think of what that thing might be. Hold it in your mind and in your heart as you read the next few pages. In fact, take it a step further and take a moment to write it out. Get a piece of paper and jot it down or pull up a note in your phone and type it out. Better yet, grab a pen and write it here in this book:

_____.

Whatever it is, be aware of it. Tune into it for a few moments.

You're not alone in having something in your life you want to shift. In fact, that's a really good sign. I'd be more concerned if you couldn't think of anything. Wanting to change something in your life is evidence of humility and strength, of maturity and growth. It tells me that you see weak spots in your life and want to get better, stronger, healthier. You want a reset.

It's why, at the beginning of every New Year, so many people come up with a list of things they want to change. Areas in which they want to get better, stronger, healthier. Some of the most common resolutions are things like exercising more, saving money, losing weight, paying off debt, traveling, and spending more time with family. You might resonate with some of those goals, but yours might even run a little deeper: wasting less time, kicking a porn habit, being less distracted and more present, having less conflict in your relationships, eating less sugar, avoiding toxic relationships, spending less money, getting more involved in church, reading more books, or something else unique to you.

The problem with trying to change is that we often approach it in the wrong way. We try to adjust or tweak a few external behaviors—waking up earlier, eating fewer calories, going to the gym, buying more books—and hope they trigger some sort of long-term effect. But a few months into the new behavior, we almost inevitably find ourselves defaulting back to old habits. It doesn't matter how old you are, your occupation or career, your socioeconomic status, race, gender, or even how long you've been a Christian. We all have old patterns we can find ourselves returning to.

The apostle Paul himself struggled with this same behavior modification problem when he said, "I do not understand what I do. For what I want to do I do not do, but what I hate I do" (Romans 7:15 NKJV). We're not alone in the struggle. Repeating the same patterns. Drawn back into the same old cycles. Paul said it this way, "I do not understand what I do." Take note of that little phrase. Because when we don't understand *why* we do what we do, we'll find ourselves doing the same things again and again. Understanding why we do what we do, learning to dig a little deeper, is paramount to changing our behavior. There's no way around it.

In my work as a licensed professional counselor, working with thousands of clients in my years of practice, it has become overwhelmingly clear that the people who end up having the most success in their attempts to change and grow are the ones who have an awareness of what's going on deep down inside, underneath the surface. When we can understand why we do what we do, we can finally begin to break free of patterns, habits, and behaviors that have been holding us back.

We all have old patterns that we can find ourselves returning to.

WHY WE DO IT

When I was in college, I owned a lemon of a car. It was a dark green Volkswagen Jetta, and I loved it so much I even named it (and no, I'm not telling you the name…because it's dorky enough to name a car, much less speak aloud its name). But the funkiest things would happen as I was driving this car. The turn signals would switch on suddenly, or the windshield wipers would start wiping, or the emergency lights would start blinking. It was quite a doozy.

One freezing cold December morning, I was in a rush to get to finals. I had hit the snooze button one too many times and was a little late getting ready that morning. I ran down the stairs and out of the building to the parking lot, pulled out my car key, and frantically put it into the door lock. As I turned the key, the windows of my car suddenly rolled down and the car alarm started blaring loudly. To make matters worse, when I pulled the keys out of the lock, the entire lock cylinder came out of the car door and was stuck to my key! Now you know how serious I was when I said I owned a lemon of a car.

There I was, in the middle of a freezing cold parking lot, trying to get the lock cylinder off my key so I could start the car and drive to my final exams. Needless to say, I ended up driving to my finals that morning in 16-degree weather with all four windows rolled down, and my car alarm blaring the whole way there. The whole situation was a hot (actually, freezing cold) mess.

But here's the thing about my lemon of a car. I was smart enough to know that duct-taping the windows, supergluing the windshield wipers, and muffling the car alarm wouldn't be the ultimate fix my car needed. Superficially changing those external issues wouldn't get to the root of the problem. I had to figure out what was going on underneath the surface if I actually wanted to turn my lemon into lemonade.

After having had enough of these funky incidents, I ended up taking my car to the shop. Turns out, my car wasn't born a lemon. Some crossed electrical wires were causing all the mishaps. You see, a few months before that, I'd asked a friend of mine to install a new stereo system for me, and it turned out he didn't really know what he was doing. He crossed some wires in the process, which eventually led to all the crazy malfunctions.

I don't know about you, but I can relate to some of that in my own life. Have you ever just tried, and tried, and tried to change—to do something different, to get something right, to do something better—and you just couldn't seem to do it? After a while, you start to think you're the problem—you're the lemon. You start wondering if there is something seriously wrong with you. Why can't you just do this one thing? Why do you feel so stuck?

Maybe there's a reason. Maybe, underneath the surface, we'll find that there are some wires crossed. I don't mean literal wires, or brain chemistry, or anything like that.[1] What I mean is this: *Somewhere along the way, what you believe got misconstrued and what you feel got misunderstood and what you did became misdirected.* And that, my friend, makes all the difference.

THOUGHTS TO FEELINGS TO BEHAVIORS

Most people go about their lives unaware of this life-changing truth: thoughts lead to feelings, and feelings lead to behaviors. That's what's going on underneath the surface, in a split second, often before you're even aware of it. This is why trying to change your life starting with external behaviors alone will usually lead you to a dead end—because you're actually starting at the end! It's trying to set boundaries without getting to the root of why you tend to say yes to everything, trying to lose weight without getting to the root of your emotional eating, or trying to stop addictively binge-watching Netflix without getting to the root of what's causing your underlying stress. Starting with external behaviors is like duct-taping the windows of my struggling Volkswagen instead of getting to the faulty wiring underneath the surface. Your thoughts are like that underlying wiring because they affect so many other parts of your body. What's happening in your mind is so key to the process of transformation and change, and knowledge of it (or lack thereof) ultimately leads to why some people succeed and others fail.

What you think leads to how you feel. Dwell in negative thinking long enough, and you'll start to feel negative. Feel negative long enough, and you'll start to default to negative behaviors. This is why so much of change happens by going underneath the surface. Getting to the roots, owning your thoughts, and understanding your feelings is what eventually leads to modifying your behaviors and ultimately changing your life. We can say it like this: thought change leads to life change.

IT'S TIME FOR A RESET

Throughout the pages of this book, we're going to go on a life-changing journey. And I mean that literally. We're going to get comfortable with going under the surface—owning our thoughts, understanding our feelings, and changing our behaviors. We're going to stop doing things the way we've done them in the past and try something new. The word *reset* means to do something differently, and that's exactly what we're going to do. We're shutting down the factory settings, the autopilot, the default mode that we've been trained to live out of for so long, and we'll replace those with something new, something better, something healthier.

Each day, you'll be introduced to a new powerful habit—a practice that offers you a short lesson and practical activity to help you shift your perspective and reset the way you've done things in the past. Each of these practices will be a life-changing psychological principle rooted in God's life-giving truths. Let me assure you right up front: these habits won't be a once-and-done thing. In fact, some of them might be ones you have to come back to for a few days, repeat a few times, and revisit in different seasons of your life. You might even find this book of practices is one you have to go through again and again through-out the ebb and flow of your life. It might even find a permanent place on your nightstand for when you need a quick refresher, you're feeling stuck, or something new pops up that you want to heal, deal with, or change. Because it's not the power of your will but the power of your practices that leads to the biggest changes in your life.

These practices are not the typical habits that you're used to, because they take you much deeper than basic external behavioral change. Some of these lessons will help you focus on owning your thoughts and beliefs, others on understanding and identifying your feelings, and others still on tuning in to why you behave the way you do. Because when your thoughts, feelings, and behaviors are in sync, working together, you'll find that change is finally attainable, growth is actually possible, and healing is truly reachable.

Since getting healthy starts from the inside out, that's exactly where we're going to start. One step at a time, one day at a time, one practice at a time. I like the word *practice* because it's a reminder that applying these strategies takes time, effort, and intention. It's not a once-and-done thing, and neither is healing, growth, and change. The process of becoming healthy is something you have to work at—something you have to practice. You don't usually get it right the first time, but it's in the practice that you see things begin to shift.

So be patient, have grace with yourself, and get yourself ready. You're choosing to say no to the status quo, the default mode, the factory setting. You're choosing to do it differently this time around. And I'm honored to be taking this journey with you.

It's time for a *reset*.

Here we go.

STOP BEFORE YOU START

PAUSE

There's a reason you picked up this book.

And the fact that you picked it up tells me a little something about you.

Because the kind of person who picks up a book like this is a person who's ready to do the work. A person who wants to make some changes in their life. A person who's ready for something new, something better, something different. A person who's curious, ready to learn. A person who's tired of trying and failing, who's ready for something different this time around. Something new. Something life changing.

And I want you to know that I like you already. You're my kind of person. The fact that you picked up this book shows me there's something different about you. You're here. You're motivated. You've showed up. You're ready to go.

You're on the starting line, ready to take off running. You get down low and put your hands on the pavement. You're waiting for your cue to start, and that epic song from *Chariots of Fire* starts playing in your head (or is that just me?). Which is why what I'm about to tell might throw off your game and mess with your head a little bit. But it has to be said.

On your mark...

Get set...

Pause!

Wait, what? Pause? Are you for real, Debra?

I know. That's not what you expected in a book where we're about to do some serious work. You're so ready to go! That intro chapter got you pumped up and ready! And just as you're about to hit Go and dive into the work of change, healing, and growth, I tell you to hit Pause.

It doesn't make sense. It seems so contradictory. Especially in our go, go, go society. "If you don't go fast and go far, you'll fall behind," they tell you. "If you stop to pause, you'll lose," they say. Pausing is so counterintuitive that we hardly do it. We see pausing as a weakness. A misstep. So, we fill our ears with noise, our minds with to-do lists, and our lives with distractions. We go, go, go—and we don't stop.

But here's what you need to understand down deep to your core before we start this whole thing: the *pause* is the start of the work. If we really want to make long-lasting changes in our lives, we have to stop before we start. We've got to take the time to hit pause, tune in. We've got to stop and listen to what God is saying, what He wants to do, and where He wants to take us. We've got to stop and make sure we're in step with Him before we go, because He knows best who we are, how we're doing, what we need, and what it looks like for us to run this race well. We have to stop so we can start well.

TUNING OUT TO TUNE IN

Have you ever fallen asleep to the TV playing in the background? Little by little, without you even realizing it's happening, your body becomes so accustomed to the background noise that you don't even hear it anymore. But here's the thing: the noise is still there. And your brain is still actively processing it. The background noise is actually wasting your energy and robbing you of a good night's sleep.

Something similar is happening to us even as we're wide awake. There can be so much activity in our lives that we don't even recognize it. Our bodies become numb to the noise. All the chaos around us is robbing us of our energy, focus, motivation, and attention without our even realizing it. Pausing is the way we reserve our energy, actively blocking out the noise so we can focus on what's going on inside us and what we want to accomplish. We're tuning out what's going on around us so we can tune in to what's going on inside of us.

There are two types of noise, two types of activity, that keep you from focusing in and being attentive. The first is *outer noise*. Outer noise is simply all the external distractions that surround us: the background music as you're exercising, the pinging ring of the text message going off in your pocket as you're having a conversation, the radio blaring in the car on the drive to work, the kids laughing or fighting or playing in the background while you're making dinner, the office chatter as you're sitting in your cubicle trying to get work done. There's outer noise all around you, and taking a deliberate pause means intentionally turning off—silencing—the noises in your immediate environment. You might turn off your ringer, switch off the music or the TV, close your computer, and be intentional about getting away somewhere quiet, just to be still.

The second type of noise is *inner noise.* This is the one that's harder to control and more intrusive at times. It's the noise of your internal thoughts buzzing around in your mind. It's the to-do list you keep mentally working through, that problem at work you keep trying to solve, the conversation you keep replaying in your head, the worries and insecurities and doubts that keep interrupting your thought process. It's your mind's tendency to wander away from the moment, whether in the middle of a conversation, when you're trying to read a book, or as you're sitting down to pray, think, or even sleep.

Being deliberate to pause, to stop, to block out the noise isn't just a suggestion. It's a necessary part of healing and change.

Pause for a moment...and listen. Hear exactly what
God wants you to change in the present, understand
where you've made mistakes in the past, and see what
you're being called to do as you look to the future.

THE POWER OF THE PAUSE

In the Bible we're introduced to Job, a man who was willing to learn, and grow, and heal. A man who was ready to rebuild his life after tragedy, loss, disappointment, and pain. And after Job had vented for a while, letting loose his own thoughts, feelings, and suggestions, God told him to "pause a moment...and listen" (Job 37:14 GNT).

Both psychology and spirituality testify to the power of the pause: the practice of stopping, of silencing the noise, of tuning in to what God is saying and what He wants to do. As one writer puts it, "Taking time to just be still and quiet gives your nervous system a chance to regain balance."[1] It gives your body and mind a chance to recalibrate, to literally reset. Science shows us that when you take the time to pause, to rest your brain from all the noise, your brain is doing some much-needed processing work.[2] It's doing some serious healing that it can't otherwise accomplish while you're in active mode. It's no wonder God specifically tells us to "Be still, and know that I am God" (Psalm 46:10). We often read this verse as a compassionate suggestion from God, a "why don't you take a minute to relax" kind of thing. But it's not a suggestion. It's much stronger, and bolder, and more candid than that. The Hebrew word here isn't a suggestion as much as it is a command.[3] Stop what you're doing. Stop. Just stop.

Cease your striving. Quit going-going-going. Take the time to pause.

Because we can't start if we've never taken the time to stop. It's not only okay to pause; it's a prerequisite to change. So, pause for a moment and listen. Hear exactly what God wants you to change in the present, understand where you've made mistakes in the past, and see what you're being called to do as you look to the future. Learn to stop before you start. And give your brain the jump-start it needs to prepare for the process of healing.

Today you have one task and one task alone: take the time to pause. On your mark, get set, pause!

VERSE FOR REFLECTION

"Pause a moment, Job, and listen. Consider the wonderful things God does" (Job 37:14 GNT).

TODAY'S HABIT: PAUSE

1. Find a quiet room, a place with little to no background noise. Turn off your phone or leave it in another room. Sit in a comfortable chair with your feet flat on the ground.

2. Close your eyes and clear your mind. Be intentional about stilling your internal thoughts. Sit quietly for ten minutes. Deeply breathe in and out, five seconds with each inhale and exhale.

3. Pray out loud or internally: *Lord, thank You that You love and care for me and want what's best for my life! I'm so grateful that You're near, and that Your presence is right here with me on the ups and downs of the journey of healing. Speak to my heart in this moment, and show me: What do You want me to shift or change in my present life? What mistakes have I made in the past that You want me to take ownership of? What are You calling me to do in an effort to heal and grow as I look to the future?*

4. After pausing for a few moments, take the time to write down what you heard, felt, or experienced. A few things to remember: ten minutes of silence *feels* a lot longer than it sounds! For many of you, this may be your first time sitting quietly with no distractions for this long. Your mind will wander, and you'll continually have to redirect it back to a posture of pausing and listening. Tune in to how you are feeling. Do any specific words or phrases come to mind?

Any themes, ideas, or thoughts? Don't panic if you don't "hear" anything right away; your brain is still doing necessary work even in the pause. It will take practice, and you may have to repeat this practice often before you can still your wandering thoughts long enough to tune into God's Spirit. Consider taking three to five minutes to make this practice part of your weekly or even daily routine.

2

SOMETHING NEW

EXPECT

Expectations often get us in trouble.

I've found that to be true in my own life as well as in the lives of my clients, especially when it comes to relationships. I'm constantly repeating: *Get your expectations right!* I'm always saying that unrealistic expectations are what get in the way of our relationships. We expect others to be perfect. We expect ourselves to get it right the first time around. We expect our closest people to always come through for us. We expect we'll never get hurt, or feel let down, or struggle through our relationships. And when those things happen, like they inevitably do because we're flawed human beings, we feel crushed, disillusioned, jaded. But one key to healthy relationships is getting our expectations right. I talk a lot about setting up realistic, healthy, flexible expectations in many of my relationship books.[1]

The problem is, I've often carried that mentality into my relationship with God. I've lowered my expectations of Him so *I* won't be disappointed, hurt, or let down. Without even being aware I was doing it, I've kept myself from putting expectations on God. I don't give Him the chance to let me down the way I've been let down in the past.

I've had some deep hurts in my past. Some major letdowns. One specific situation comes to mind where I cried out to God from the depths of my heart and from one of the deepest points of pain for something specific to happen…and it didn't happen. At least not in the way I had asked. I felt let down, hurt, and even a little betrayed. So, I started interacting with God the way I interact with others: as though He's a flawed human being who can't always be trusted to come through for me. I lowered my expectations of Him. I brought Him to a place of humanity rather than a place of sovereignty. But you know what? In trying to save myself from pain, I ended up suffering more in the end. It was my loss.

Because I stopped expecting great things of God. I stopped asking great things of God. I stopped believing for great things from God. Because I was afraid to ask, to believe, to expect, I missed out on so many great things He wanted to do.

Maybe you too have lowered your expectations of God because of past hurt, pain, or disappointments. Maybe deep down, you've stopped actually believing that He can do it, or that He can help *you* do it, and instead started believing that if you want something done, you have to be the one to do it. But what if, in our own efforts at preserving our hearts, we've allowed our hearts to atrophy?

Because to stop believing is to stop living.

LITTLE FAITH, BIG GOD

My five-year-old son recently had an elaborate four-hour surgery scheduled. Not just the surgery but the recovery was going to be really brutal on him. As his mom, I hated it. I wanted so badly for the surgery to go well, and I was praying for that every day.

One day, as I was praying, I felt in my spirit that I needed to pray that he wouldn't have to have the surgery. To be honest, I thought it was a ridiculous thing to pray, because I knew he had to have this surgery to avoid long-term complications. It had to happen. Not only that, but I'd been let down asking God for big things in the past, so it felt a little foolish to pray for something this big. I didn't want to put that on God. I didn't want to end up disappointed. But this prompting inside me wouldn't go away, so I prayed earnestly. I asked God to intervene.

I asked specifically that the surgery wouldn't be necessary. And then I moved on with the day and got everything ready for the next day's trip to the operating center.

We got to the OR early the next morning with our very anxious five-year-old. They checked us in and then we distracted him as best as we could while we waited for him to be taken back to the operating area. Finally, it was his turn. We said our goodbyes and encouraged him to be brave as the medical staff took him back on a stretcher. One of us had to stay in the waiting area for the next four-plus hours, so we decided to take turns. I quickly went out for a coffee run to try to distract myself from the long, miserable, second-by-second tick-tocking of that slow, relentless clock.

About 40 minutes later, my phone rang. It was my husband—with the surgeon on speaker phone. My heart sank. What had happened in the middle of surgery? Being the wife of a surgeon myself, I know that surgeons don't come out of the OR and break scrub unless something serious happens. "Everything's okay, hon," John quickly assured me, knowing that I was probably panicking at this point. "Dr. D. just wants to talk to us." The doctor went on to explain that after going in with a scope, the problem that the scans had shown urgently needed repair was no longer there. He didn't think our son would need this surgery after all. All that was left was to wait for the anesthesia to wear off.

I instantly started to cry. My mind was blown. How could this even be possible? How could this even be real? I prayed for this, but the fact that it actually happened was too much for my tiny faith to compute. The words of Jesus from Matthew 8:26 ran through my head, "You of little faith, why are you so afraid?" Here I was, witnessing a miracle. Not because of who I am or what I did or didn't do, but because of who God is.

I'm on a journey of increasing my expectations of God. He's not a flawed human being who will let me down; He's the almighty God who raises me up, calls me higher, and knows what's best for me even when it doesn't match my plans. I've seen Him perform miracles, heal me from depression, empower me to overcome my anxiety, restore my body after a tragic loss, and use my story to bless thousands of other people. When it comes to asking and expecting things of God, I'm learning to increase my expectations. My friend and spiritual mentor Christine Caine said to me once in a conversation, "You ask Him for *everything*, and you let Him decide what He does or doesn't do!" And it stuck with me. His plans are higher than mine (Isaiah 55:8-9).

> When it comes to asking and expecting things of God, I'm learning to increase my expectations.

SELF-FULFILLING PROPHECY

In counseling and psychology, a "self-fulfilling prophecy" means that sometimes, when we believe or expect something to happen, we unconsciously (and sometimes even consciously) act in a way to make that thing happen. If I wake up believing that today is going to be a great day, I'll likely do things to influence that great day becoming a reality. I'll start the day with a smile on my face, be kinder to the people I run into, look for the good things and be grateful about the small things. But if I start the day believing it will be terrible, I'll likely find that to be true as well.

The concept of self-fulfilling prophecy shows us how much influence we have in the way we see the world, and in turn, how we behave as a result. It's the same way with our expectations. What we expect—both of God and of ourselves—is often what we'll begin to see. If I expect that God is good, and mighty, and powerful and sovereign, I'm going to begin to experience Him in those ways because my eyes are looking for His goodness. If I expect that I am capable of change, healing, and growth, I'm going to make decisions that lead in those directions. What we expect, therefore, determines much of how we live. Much of how we change. Much of how we heal.

First John 5:14 reminds us of the posture of expectation we should have: "This is the confidence we have in approaching God: that if we ask anything according to his will, he hears us." We can ask God for great things. Big things. Bold things. For hearts to be healed and lives to be changed; for generational chains to break, families to be restored, and marriages to be renewed. God is doing something new in your life. In fact, He's already begun. The questions are: Do we believe it? Do we receive it? Do we expect it? Are we looking for it? Are we even ready for it?

VERSE FOR REFLECTION

"I am about to do something new. See, I have already begun! Do you not see it?" (Isaiah 43:19 NLT).

TODAY'S HABIT: EXPECT

1. Is there an area of your life where you've felt let down by God or others? How has this affected your ability to expect and believe?

2. On a scale of one to ten (ten being the highest), how do you rate your "expectations" of God, believing in His promises and power? On a scale of one to ten, how would you rate your expectations of change, healing, and growth in your personal life?

3. In what area could God be asking you to expect change this
   coming year? On a notecard, write down three areas where
   you are asking *and expecting* God to work, in your personal
   life, your family, your relationships, your work, and your
   health.[2]

4. Put your list of expectations somewhere you will see it daily.
   Commit to praying over these specific things on a regular
   basis.

3

OWN YOUR JUNK

ACKNOWLEDGE

D o you want to know the one thing that's holding you back, keeping you stuck, and preventing you from change?

It's you.

You are that thing. And not because you want to be. Not because you're trying to be. But because you see yourself from the inside out rather than the outside in. Human beings have an uncanny ability to see themselves as better than they really are.

I started my book *Are You Really OK?* with the presumptuous sentence, "You're not as healthy as you think you are." I went on to explain the better-than-average-effect, a social experiment where people were asked to rate themselves on a scale compared to their peers in different aspects of life.[1] Sure enough, the majority of people rated themselves as *better than average*. But mathematically, that doesn't compute. We can't all be better than average. Someone has to fall below the mean. The problem is, it's hard to acknowledge that this someone is actually me. We have a tendency to see ourselves through a biased lens.

Jesus reminds us that it's so much easier to see the flaws of others than it is to see our own when He says, "How can you say to your brother, 'Let me take the speck out of your eye,' when all the time there is a plank in your own eye? You hypocrite, first take the plank out of your own eye, and then you will see clearly to remove the speck from your brother's eye" (Matthew 7:4-5).

Because we see ourselves so subjectively, we tend to have blind spots. It can be hard to pinpoint what we need to change, or even see a serious need for change at all. And that is what ultimately holds us back. But any counselor, psychologist, or behavioral specialist will tell you that the first step to change is acknowledging that something needs to change. In other words, owning your junk.

OUTSIDE-IN PERSPECTIVE

You've had a little time to think about it so far, but today I want to offer you a different exercise. I want you to stop looking at yourself from the inside out and try to see yourself from the outside in. How do other people see you? Think about the most recent conflict, argument, or interaction you had and ask yourself this: What was the other person's perspective of you? Try to view it like you would a movie scene, two people interacting. See yourself from the outside looking in. What do you observe about yourself? What do you notice about your tone, volume, body language, and the words you speak? How is the other person responding to you?

This is just an example of learning to see a situation from the outside in. Practicing objectivity in how you see yourself is an important habit because it gives you a chance to take notice of your blind spots and deal with them. If you're walking around with a big ol' plank in your eye, your vision of yourself and others is going to be skewed.

I wonder if that plank Jesus refers to is simply our personal bias—our ability to judge others more quickly than our willingness to assess and take inventory of ourselves. Failing to do so prevents us from true healing. According to James 5:16, the first step to healing is this: "Confess your sins to each other." In other words, own your junk. Recognize it and speak it aloud.

"I ADMIT"

Twelve-step groups, such as Alcoholics Anonymous or Celebrate Recovery, are some of the most effective ways of moving toward addiction recovery. The recovery groups follow 12 steps that help them move toward change, starting with this crucial first step that says: *We admitted we were powerless over our addictions and compulsive behaviors, that our lives had become unmanageable.* Do you see a remarkable pattern here? Both psychology and Scripture point to the exact same thing: Acknowledging your sins, struggles, and weaknesses is the first step to healing.

With confession comes freedom.

It's much easier to see what needs to change around us and what needs to change in others than to see what needs to change in ourselves. But how much healthier would we be if we could stop on a regular basis and take ownership of our own junk? How much more clearly could we see life if we would only take the plank out of our own eyes? We can't change anyone or anything but ourselves. So if you really want to change your community, your church, your marriage, your family, or your world, start with the one person you can actually impact the most. Start with yourself.

VERSE FOR REFLECTION

"Confess your sins to each other and pray for each other so that you may be healed" (James 5:16).

TODAY'S HABIT: ACKNOWLEDGE

Set aside ten minutes today to practice objectivity.

1. Look at your life as though you're watching a movie and you're the main character. Imagine yourself going through the motions of a typical 24-hour period.

2. Observe your daily habits, interactions, and behaviors. What do you do at the start and end of the day? What do you do when you feel stressed out? What are your interactions and conversations with others like? What does your body language say? How do you spend your time? Take a few minutes to write down some observations of yourself as you imagine your day.

3. Looking at yourself objectively, what would you tell that person they needed to change? What do they need to work on? How can they improve their relationships? Are there any unhealthy habits they need to adjust? How can they grow and mature in emotional health, spiritual health, mental health, physical health, or even relational health?

4. Based on today's practice, write down one thing you want to change in this season of your life. By writing it down you are taking the step to acknowledge and confess it: _____ _____. Take a few moments to say it out loud to yourself, and then spend some time confessing it to God in prayer. Think of one person with whom you can share this specific thing you would like to change and write their name down.

4

WHY NOW?

DECIDE

W hy now?

That's a question I often ask my clients early in the therapy process. After we get to the bottom of what they're there for and what they want to work on, the next question is, *why*? Why do you want to work on this now? What's happening in your life that's pushed you to want to make a change? In other words, why now?

"Because I'm tired of getting hurt in the end. I'm tired of giving, and giving, and getting nothing back in return. I've realized that I'm 50 percent of the equation of my unhealthy relationships, and I need to do something about it." That was the "why now" answer Melissa gave me in one of our sessions recently.

"Because I'm going to lose my marriage if things don't change. I keep falling back into the same habits of anger and rage, not communicating well, having all these feelings bottled up inside, and feeling stuck. I'm pushing my wife and family away, and I'm feeling more isolated than ever before. I need to stop blaming everyone else. I need to change before it's too late." That "why now" answer from Clayton clued me in to how badly he wanted this.

"Because I'm not enjoying life anymore. I'm stressed out all the time, I have way too much on my plate, and I feel completely burnt out. I kept trying to push through, hoping something would change, but I'm realizing it won't change unless I change it. I want to enjoy life, not just feel like I have to get through it." That was the "why now" Andrea shared before we started her healing journey.

Why now? It's a really important question for those of us who have something in our lives we want to change, because it helps us get to the bottom of how much we really want it. *What is this worth to me right now? What am I willing to give up for it? Do I want to make this change right now? Am I ready to make this change? Why am I deciding to change this behavior now? What's at stake if I don't?* Your answer to those questions is an important step in determining whether change is actually around the corner.

In order to see a shift or change in your life, you need more reasons to work for change than reasons to stay still. You have to want healing more than you want comfort. Because frankly, it's more comfortable to stay the same. Staying the same is the easier option. Maybe this is the reason Jesus asked the paralytic if he wanted to be healed *before* He healed him (John 5:6)—because the *why* is the foundation of healing.

To see a shift or change in your life, you need more
reasons to work for change than reasons to stay still.

THE *WHY* OF HEALING

You see, there's a reason we continue to do what we continue to do. Every behavior gives us some sort of benefit—a reward, if you will. Even the most seemingly dysfunctional behaviors offer us some sort of a benefit; otherwise we wouldn't keep doing them. We eat the thousand extra calories because the food tastes good and gives us comfort. We explode in anger because rage makes us feel in control and powerful. We take that additional drink because alcohol decreases our stress and numbs our pain. We date that toxic person because he makes us feel wanted and silences the loneliness.

There is always a reward attached to our behavior, even if that reward causes us more harm than good in the end. And we're not just talking a physical reward; there's an internal reward motivating us behind the scenes. Science has revealed a "reward response" reaction inside our bodies, meaning our brains release dopamine (the feel-good chemical) whenever we're exposed to a rewarding stimulus, sending a surge of pleasure to our bodies. We physically and emotionally respond to rewards. And so, as long as there's some sort of reward, we will continue to do that behavior, engage in that relationship, follow that pattern of interaction.

But here's the simple yet profound truth: For us to really change, the benefits of changing have to become greater than the benefits of staying the same. The reward has to flip to the other side. What we want to do, to change, or fix has to become more rewarding than what we're currently doing.

It sounds easy, but this perspective shift takes intention, will, effort, and practice. In counseling, we call this the *contemplation stage* of change. After first realizing there's a problem, it's the stage of change where we really get to the bottom of why we want to change and determine that our current habits, behaviors, interactions, and patterns are causing more harm than good. In other words, we're really considering the cost of changing versus staying the same. We're thinking long and hard about it. And the scale is finally tipping in the direction of change.

But believe it or not, contemplation is actually the second stage of change. So then what's the first stage of change, you might ask? Well, it's the stage before you picked up this book. Before you decided you needed a reset. It's called pre-contemplation. In that first stage, the behavior you want to change still seems to be more desirable than change itself. That slice of cake is more desirable than your physical health. That extra 15 minutes of sleep is more desirable than 15 minutes in God's Word. That sexual fantasy is more desirable than authenticity with your spouse. But now, we're in contemplation stage, and things are starting to shift. We're starting to change the way we see our lives and our behaviors. Our perspective is transforming so we no longer see the behavior as the reward, but the possibility of changing as the reward. Because the reward is *in* the change.

Being healthy, strong, and at our ideal weight becomes more desirable than that slice of cake. Getting filled up and refreshed by God's Word, more desirable than a little extra sleep. Enjoying deep intimacy with our spouse, more desirable than the temporary rush of porn. The reward has shifted to the other side. Your brain begins to respond to the new perceived reward. And now it's more desirable than the unhealthy behavior.

It takes work to get to this phase of change—mental work. We've got to start changing the way we see our behavior, stacking the pile in favor of change, being intentional to identify the ways in which *not* changing is holding us back. We've got to take a serious look at the question Jesus posed to the paralytic at the pool of Bethesda: "Do you want to get well?" And then we have to ask the same question of ourselves.

Do I want to be healed?
Do I want to change?
Why?
Why now?

If we can tip the scale in the direction of change, if we can answer with a resounding, "Yes, I really want to get well!" and conceptualize *why* change is better than staying the same, we're one huge step closer to getting there. Because making the decision to change is half the battle.

VERSE FOR REFLECTION

"Do you want to be healed?" (John 5:6 ESV).

TODAY'S HABIT: DECIDE

1. Take a moment to imagine Jesus asking you this very personal question, "Do you want to be healed?" Think about it before answering right away. How do you answer that question?

2. When you're in the pre-contemplation stage, whatever you want to change tends to come with some sort of reward. Make an honest list of the rewards you get from engaging in your current pattern. Try to identify five reasons why this pattern (or behavior, interaction, relationship, and the like) has been desirable to you. What is the reward that makes you keep doing it?

3. Now that you're moving into contemplation stage, make a list of the "rewards" you'll get from changing your behavior. These are the *why* of why you want to change. Try to identify at least ten reasons you want to change. For example, the person who desires to eat well and exercise might write:

   Because I want to be healthy.

   Because I want to honor God with my body.

   Because it feels so good to be healthy.

   Because I want to go to God to fill me up emotionally rather than food.

Because I'm tired of the afternoon sugar crash.

Because I want to become physically stronger (and so forth).

Take your time to add to this list and come back and visit it every few days or anytime you need a shift in perspective or a reminder of where you're going and why you want to get there.

5

THE DEEP END

CHECK IN WITH YOUR EMOTIONS

My husband says I could stay in the deep end for hours. He says I'm like an Olympic swimmer. But he's definitely not talking about the pool; he's talking about my tolerance of emotional interactions and expression. Because emotions are deep, and *your* emotions are a really deep and meaningful part of who you are.

I often explain this idea by talking about the three levels of conversation. *Facts* are the first and most superficial level because they're easier to talk about (that's like the shallow end where the water comes up to your waist). *Opinions and ideas* take you a little deeper in conversation and offer a little more of who you are (now we're in a little deeper, but if you stand on your tiptoes, you're still touching the bottom of the pool). And *feelings* are the very deepest and most vulnerable part of you (we're in the deep end now, where you've got to know how to swim to make it).

Again, I'm pretty comfortable swimming in the deep end. My husband, John, on the other hand, says when it comes to emotional exchanges, he feels like a three-year-old wrapped in his ducky floaty, comfortable and content hanging out in the shallow end all day.

There are reasons we both have different comfort levels when it comes to emotional interaction and expression. He comes from a background where deep, emotional conversations weren't part of his regular day-to-day life. Even though spiritual conversations were routine (theology, Bible, apologetics), emotional conversations weren't. Sometimes we confuse spiritual and emotional conversations and think they're one and the same. But they're not. John was more than comfortable talking about *God;* he just wasn't comfortable talking about *himself*—his own feelings, emotions, and needs. He never learned how to swim in the deep parts of who he was and how he felt. So he stuffed down his feelings and stuck to facts, theology, apologetics, and even opinions and debates. The logical exchanges just felt more comfortable.

I think I was forced into the deep end just by the sheer nature of my life and circumstances. I was always that friend with whom everyone shared the hard stuff. Even adults in my life came to me with their emotional needs. I learned to get comfortable with the deep end pretty quickly. Not only that, but my work as a therapist has given me the practice I needed to dive into those deep waters for myself. That's the thing we all need to understand: being comfortable with the deepest part of our hearts has nothing to do with our personality or gender but everything to do with our experiences.

Just like swimming in a pool, we've got to practice going deep with our emotions to get better at feeling, understanding, and expressing them. It's not something you're born knowing how to do; it's something you have to learn along the way.

If you don't check in, you'll eventually check out.

THE DEEP END

Going deep and checking in with how you're really feeling is harder for some than for others. Maybe you grew up in a family where conversations tended to stay superficial, and so that became your comfort level. Or maybe you came from a background where showing emotions actually made you look weak, where phrases like "Stop crying or I'll give you something to cry about," or "There's no need to get emotional about this," were the norm. Maybe you felt the need to stuff your emotions in order to be accepted, loved, or respected. Or maybe you come from a background of really hard things like trauma, abuse, or family dysfunction or violence. Sometimes, in those really hard situations, our bodies learn to mute their ability to feel deep emotions for a while so we can survive those experiences.

I recently had a conversation with a ministry leader who told me he doesn't really have many emotions. Maybe it's a "man thing," he wondered. But as we discussed further, he opened up about the rough childhood he had. Abandoned by his father, abused by his mother, his body learned to block out emotions because they were just so hard. And now, 40 years later, even in an environment of safety and security, his body has stayed in that default mode. He doesn't feel as easily as the next person, not because it's a "man thing," but because that's how he survived so many hard years.

Maybe you can relate. For one reason or another, you've learned to block out your emotions—or at least quiet them down a bit. They're there, but the volume has been turned down really low. You try not to visit the deep end of emotions; you'd rather stay in the comfort and contentment of the shallow end. But here's the thing: If you don't check in, you'll eventually check out. If you don't take the time to go deep and see how you're really doing from the inside out, eventually all those feelings you've been stuffing will come to the surface in an unexpected way. If you don't take the time to deal with your emotions, they will deal with you. And many times, those undealt-with emotions, brewing just under the surface of your life, are the very thing keeping you from healing and freedom and victory in your life.

Scripture says, "The purposes of a person's heart are deep waters, but one who has insight draws them out" (Proverbs 20:5). In other words, the reasons we do what we do are rooted deep inside us. You've got to draw them out. You've got to go in and do the work of bringing up what's going on inside you so you can face it, deal with it, and heal it. That's what it means to be a person of "in-sight." You have the sight to see what's going on inside you. You take the time to look in, to check in, and to draw it out.

It's time to say goodbye to the floaties in the shallow end. Because we're about to learn how to swim. We're jumping in the deep end.

VERSE FOR REFLECTION

"The purposes of a person's heart are deep waters, but one who has insight draws them out" (Proverbs 20:5).

TODAY'S HABIT: CHECK IN WITH YOUR EMOTIONS

1. Before we check in today, get yourself to a comfortable quiet place.

   Close your eyes and picture in your mind the deep end of the pool or an ocean or a body of water. From the view above, it's hard to see what's at the very bottom. Imagine that deepest part is your emotional world.

2. Let's dive in for a few moments. What's going on deep inside you? How comfortable is it for you to tap into your emotions? How often do you take the time to go down to this deeper level of who you are? What are some things that might make this difficult for you to do?

3. What are some feelings you've experienced over the last 24 hours? What (or who) has caused those feelings? How have you reacted to those feelings today?

4. What are some of the feelings you've experienced over the last three to six months? What might be the source of some of those feelings? Is there one that keeps coming up again and again? How do you tend to deal with uncomfortable or difficult emotions?

5. Maybe you're having a hard time figuring out what you feel or just aren't sure. If so, imagine yourself swimming deep down in the deep end, and ask God to reveal to you the emotions or experiences that may be buried deep down inside. Consider teaming up with a licensed counselor to help you go deep or face any obstacles or past experiences that might be keeping you from your emotional world. (See Appendix B, and go to www.DebraFileta.com/counseling/ for counselor recommendations and resources and the opportunity to connect with me and my team at the Debra Fileta Counselors Network.)

6

PLAN IT OUT

PREPARE FOR CHANGE

Y ou can learn a lot about life, people, and personalities from building IKEA furniture.

There are two types of people when it comes to building these affordable pieces of furniture that come in about 1.2 million tiny pieces. The first type of person is my husband. He's the planner. I'll even go so far as calling him an *overplanner* (yeah, I said it). First, he carefully opens the box (and by carefully, I mean surgeon style, go figure), slowly taking every single piece out while checking and rechecking it for the slightest evidence of damage. Next, he organizes them in alphabetical order based on their little microscopic stickers. Then he opens every bag of screws and puts each type into a pile with its own kind. After that, he lines up all the tools he needs in their own spaces. Then he gets out the instructions and begins working through them page by page. It feels like he's getting ready to build some sort of magnificent ark, and I'm expecting the animals to start lining up in front of our house, two by two. In the amount of time it takes him to build a bookshelf, I could have written two more books.

But then there's me. The *underplanner*. I'm efficient to the point of cutting corners if I need to. All that hype seems like a waste of time when you can just get into it. I tear open the box, quickly pull out all the pieces (not even thinking about damage and probably even causing damage in the process), rip open the bags and dump out the screws into a pile, and then see what I can accomplish on my own before wasting my time fiddling with the instructions. I mean, how hard can it be to build this bookshelf anyway? (Famous last words.)

Here's the thing: both the overplanner and the underplanner have their own set of obstacles—in IKEA furniture and in life.

Sometimes you can get so bogged down by the details of the instructions, so overwhelmed by requirements, so burdened by tasks you need to do, that you get paralyzed in the process. You analyze and overanalyze, plan and overplan, and when it's time to do the work you're too exhausted from the prelude. You're too overwhelmed to even get started.

But then there are those who just like to wing it. You don't feel like you need a plan, so you just go for it, freestyle. You're led by impulse, or passion, or the heat of the moment. But eventually, that passion runs out. And without the proper plan in place, you lose steam, resources, and motivation. You give up, defaulting to old patterns and old habits.

I don't know if you can relate to either side of the spectrum, but if we really want to make progress in our lives, we've got to find ourselves somewhere in the middle. Having a plan is an important part of moving forward in your life. As the adage goes, "If you fail to prepare you are preparing to fail." All over Scripture we're reminded to plan and prepare, but at the same time we're balanced by the truth that while we can plan and overplan, the Lord is the One who ultimately maps out our course (Proverbs 16:9). The balance comes in doing our part and trusting God with the rest.

When it comes to doing our part, having a plan in place is essential. Action itself is not enough. What happens *before* we take action is often what sets us up for success. Preparing for change is saying you're ready to receive it.

- Maybe it means making a plan to clean out your pantry and refrigerator and then meal planning and grocery shopping for healthy alternatives.

- Maybe it means setting up an easy-to-follow exercise schedule and investing in some equipment to get you started.

- Maybe it means mapping out your calendar and setting aside time for rest and recovery to avoid burnout.

- Maybe it means coming up with ways to intentionally replace those pockets of time when you tend to default to harmful habits and behaviors with ideas for new life-giving activities instead.

- Maybe it means coming up with a detailed list of reasons you aren't going to pick up the phone when that toxic ex tries reaching out.

Whatever it looks like for you, the key is to have a plan. Before you can do something differently, you've got to map it out differently. In fact, the third stage of change is just that: preparation. First, you're in precontemplation (not quite seeing the need for change); next you enter contemplation (where you start weighing the risks and rewards of change, leaning toward changing); and finally, when you make the decision to change, you enter the stage of preparation. So many people skip this stage and want to jump from deciding to change to acting on change. But it doesn't work.

Preparing for change is saying you're ready to receive it.

HOW TO FAIL

Preparation is a crucial step. The success or failure of your ability to act on your desire for change hinges on how much you've prepared for it. This stage is sometimes referred to as the "determination stage," because how much you prepare for change shows how *determined* you are to change. Too many people take this step too lightly, quickly, or haphazardly, deciding they want to change something in their lives but falling flat on their faces because they haven't considered what it will take to make that change happen. You don't decide today that you want to run a marathon and expect to be able to run it by tomorrow. In fact, you're literally setting yourself up for failure without taking the time to prepare. I promise you: *you will fail.* Wanting it badly enough won't magically get you to a better place. You've got to prepare for change whether small or significant.

> If you want to save your marriage, you've got to prepare.
>
> If you want to kick porn, you've got to prepare.
>
> If you want to get healthy, you've got to prepare.
>
> If you want to control your anger, you've got to prepare.
>
> If you want an organized home, you've got to prepare.
>
> If you want to be a better parent, you've got to prepare.
>
> If you want to decrease stress in your life, you've got to prepare.

No matter what you want to change, adjust, strengthen, or fix in your life, you're going to have to spend some time preparing. The very science of human behavior mapped out through the stages of change confirms this to be a reality, but so does God's Word! From the Israelites in the Old Testament all the way to the apostles in the New Testament, God encouraged His people to prepare and plan ahead: "Be ready" (Matthew 24:44 ESV), "Always be prepared" (1 Peter 3:15 ESV), "Be ready in season and out of season" (2 Timothy 4:2 ESV).

I could have chosen so many different passages of Scripture for reflection today, but this one in Proverbs maps it out so clearly: You've got to get everything ready before you build that house. Have the tools, equipment, and support that you need *first,* and then get to work building something new. If we're believing for change—and we are!— let's prepare for change.

"Prepare your work outside; get everything ready for yourself in the field, and after that build your house" (Proverbs 24:27 ESV).

TODAY'S HABIT: PREPARE FOR CHANGE

1. On the scale of overplanning (ten) to underplanning (zero), where do you tend to fall on the spectrum when it comes to moving toward a goal? Give an example of a situation in which you over- or underplanned. How did it play out?

2. Write out the one thing you would like to change, work on, or shift in this season of life:

3. *Prepare.* Come up with a plan for change. Write down at least five things you need to do to make that change happen. Think of tools, supports, accountability, and lifestyle changes, as well as when you will do those things. Note: Focus your plan for change on only one behavior or habit or area of growth at a time. Choose one area you want to change, or else you'll become overwhelmed. It's often helpful to give yourself a timeframe to accomplish each point. The most significant changes happen when you begin to prepare and then implement the plan within one month of writing it out. Realize that sometimes you will map out your

plan and find that something doesn't work out the way you thought it would. When that happens, come back to your plan and make any necessary adjustments or alterations. Try again until you find something that works. This might be something you have to come back to again and again as you're mapping out changes in your life.

7

IT'S NOT A ONE-PLAYER GAME

ASK FOR HELP

I s it hard for you to ask for help?

I asked that question in my Instagram stories, and I was struck by the consistency in the answers I received. Most people answered with a resounding, "Yes, it's really hard to ask for help." When we dug a little deeper and asked why it was so hard, here's what people said:

- "I'm afraid to trust other people. I'm afraid of being disappointed and rejected if they find out who I really am."

- "I'm afraid of being judged. It hurts my ego so much. I feel like I should figure it out on my own, and it's hard to admit I can't do it."

- "I'm slow to recognize that I need help. I didn't have support growing up, so I feel like I have to do it on my own."

- "I don't want to be a burden. I'm afraid to inconvenience other people because I feel like I'm not worth being helped."

While so many insightful answers came up regarding why we don't ask for help, I noticed a clear theme that emerged in the answers. *Fear*. Fear of rejection, fear of being exposed, fear of disappointment, fear of trusting others, fear of being judged, fear of vulnerability, fear of being a burden. It's amazing how much fear we have underneath the surface, motivating us to do what we do (or even what we choose *not* to do, in this case). Not only that, but because asking for help elicits such internal fears, it activates the same regions of our brain as physical pain.[1] We can literally say that it "pains" some people to ask for help.

Because of all these underlying fears we're fighting deep down inside, asking for help becomes an act of faith. We must recognize the fears so we can silence them and move forward in faith. God tells us to ask. He tells us to ask for help, and to ask for what we need. And He reminds us that those who ask, receive. Just as much faith goes into asking as into believing we will receive. And maybe, just maybe, choosing not to ask is choosing to live in fear.

Just as much faith goes into asking as
into believing that we will receive.

IT'S NOT A ONE-PLAYER GAME

I don't think I've ever accomplished anything of value without asking for help both from God and from others. I've learned not to be afraid to admit that I can't do it all on my own—because I've tried and failed numerous times in my life. The fear of asking limits us not only from accomplishment and success but from growth, from deeper intimacy with others, from trust, from vulnerability, and even from healing.

God clearly saw that it was not good for man to be alone, so He created others to fill that void (Genesis 2:18). It's true that many times, we've been hurt along the way—betrayed, abandoned, and let down—but that doesn't mean we should allow those past hurts to hold us back from creating new experiences. We need to learn to recognize our needs and desires and our shortcomings and ask for help with them. Help from God and help from others.

As we've seen, one of the reasons we fail to ask for help is that we're afraid the request will be rejected. We're afraid the person we're asking will be too busy, annoyed by our request, unwilling to help, or unavailable. Social psychologists call this a "failure of perspective-taking," because we're more focused on the reasons they might say no than our own need. No one wants to be a bother, and we're afraid the person we're approaching will see our request as an imposition. But there's another perspective to consider. Most people want to say yes when given an opportunity to help. It's rewarding for them and offers them the chance to feel connected. Not only that, but studies show that when we ask, people will often give us better quality help than we even expected. Don't underestimate how eager people are to provide support.[2]

Another reason we fail to ask for help is because we've been rejected before. We carry some of those wounds with us and allow them to influence how we act and react going forward. Sometimes when you get rejected once, you decide to give up altogether and never ask again. It can be easy to assume the worst in why the other person said no or in why they failed to respond to your need for help. Your assumptions can cause you to back away, feel embarrassed or hurt, and decide that it wasn't worth asking. But often, we're making assumptions that may not be based on reality. "Research shows that people who have rejected you in the past are actually more likely to help you than other people. When I reject you and you offer me another opportunity to help, if I can, I jump at it. I want to feel better. I want to repair the relationship. It's this big untapped resource that a lot of people have."[3] So much of what is keeping us from asking for help are battles we've got to fight in our mind first and foremost—assumptions that keep us from reaching out, connecting, and getting the help that we need, and thought processes that might not even be based on reality.

Getting to the Ask

As we're getting ready to make the ask for help, let's take a moment to map it out. Is there an area in your life right now where you need help? We'll call this *the problem*. You can usually tell because it's an area marked by feelings of frustration, exhaustion, bitterness, resentment, or repeated failure. It's that problem spot that keeps coming up again and again. When you get to the point where you're experiencing those things, it's a sign that you probably should have asked for help a long time ago—even before you got to this place of feeling stuck. Because frustration is usually the mark of an unfulfilled need.

Next, take some time to specifically identify *the need*. What is it that you actually need help with? What would bring relief, support, and encouragement in this situation? It's often easier to both ask for help and receive it when we have a specific need we can put into words. You may have even heard friends or family say, "Let me know if there's anything you need," but have you ever considered giving them an actual need? People are willing to help; they could just use a little direction. Maybe the need is help around the house, watching your kids during the week, a home-cooked meal, some advice or counsel, financial aid, help alleviating the workload, a ride to a doctor's appointment, accountability, or some other need very specific to your situation. Put it into words so you're ready to make the ask.

Third, take some time to think through *the person*. Who might be the right person to ask for help? Think through the circle of people in your life whom you could ask. Don't prematurely make excuses of why they might say no, but instead think through the fact that they might be available, willing, and wanting to help. Remember, people are far more willing to help than we often realize.

Last, consider *the ask*. How, when, and where can you ask for this need to be met? Will you make a phone call, see this person during the week, or even send a text asking for help? Decide how you'll make the ask and give yourself a timeframe to make it. When you lay out the details and map out your ask, it's much more likely to happen.

Whether you're just entering a season of needing additional help and support or you've been there for quite a while, here's the good news:

It's not too late. It's never too late. The promise still stands. Ask, and it will be given to you. Seek, and you will find. Knock, and the door will be opened. But here's the thing: it takes choosing faith over fear. Life is not a one-player game, so be sure to ask for help along the way.

VERSE FOR REFLECTION

"Ask and it will be given to you; seek and you will find; knock and the door will be opened to you" (Matthew 7:7).

TODAY'S HABIT: ASK FOR HELP

1. Is it hard for you to ask for help? Why? Reread the list at the beginning of this chapter and write your own worries or hesitations.

2. *The problem:* In what areas of your life are you feeling frustration, exhaustion, bitterness, resentment, or a general pattern of repeated failure?

3. *The need:* Under each one of those areas, write down the specific need or desire you have.

4. *The person:* Who could you ask for help?

5. *The ask:* What is one way you can ask for help with that need?

DEFAULT MODE

DO IT DIFFERENTLY

Without your awareness, your thoughts are controlling your life. They're the little messages going on in your mind throughout the day that help you interpret the world around you. They're the words you tell yourself to help you define and make sense of your experiences. Thoughts are powerful, because they shape your beliefs, which in turn influence your feelings, which in turn dictate your behavior. It's worth saying again: *Thoughts lead to feelings, which lead to behavior.* If there's any hope of significantly changing a behavior, response, or reaction in your life, you've got to start with understanding the thoughts fueling those behaviors.[1]

THE ABCS OF THERAPY

The first three letters of the alphabet can be much more life changing than you ever realized, because in counseling, the ABCs of therapy are a helpful way to understand how thoughts influence behaviors.[2] The A stands for the "activating event." This is the experience that triggers the negative, harmful, or irrational thoughts. For example, your boss brings up a project you're working on and asks if you've completed it. Your husband tells you he really doesn't want to be late to church this morning and asks you not to delay. Or your friend brings up a recent outing with another group of friends that you didn't know about.

Here's how you recognize an activating event (A) in your life: It leads to a flurry of negative and even irrational thoughts. This is the next part of the cycle (B): Your *beliefs* about the event. They're the thoughts that follow the activating event, such as:

- *Does he not realize how hard I'm working on this project? He must think I'm not working fast enough. He thinks I'm the laziest employee around. I'm not measuring up to his standards. I bet he's thinking of replacing me.*

- *He's ignoring everything I did this morning for our family! Doesn't he see how hard I work and how much I do? I'm so underappreciated in this house. My husband doesn't even care about me.*

- *I can't believe no one invited me! There must be something about me they don't like. I knew I wasn't good enough for this group of people. They probably all hate me and they're just pretending to be my friends.*

The thing to remember is, these thoughts and beliefs aren't always extremely negative and irrational like the thoughts above; they're just negative enough to start taking your mind and heart to places you don't want to go. The other thing to remember about negative thoughts is that you'll often feel justified in thinking them. You might not even recognize how negative and unhealthy they are because you're so used to thinking that way.

Our brains are really good at taking the path of least resistance. Your brain is going to find itself thinking the easiest thoughts to think, and 100 percent of the time, the easiest thoughts to think are the negative thoughts. In fact, these thoughts happen so quickly, so automatically, we often fail to recognize them. It takes real effort and intention to catch those negative thoughts and actually do something about them. (We'll talk in depth about this in the next daily step.)

Next in the ABC model comes the letter C: the consequence. The activating event led to a belief (a flurry of negative thinking), which leads to the consequence of a negative feeling. The feeling could be anything from sadness to frustration to insecurity to shame to embarrassment. But here's the thing to note: it's a *negative* feeling because of the *negative* thoughts that came before it! Again, thoughts lead to feelings, which then lead to behaviors. Because what do you do when you're feeling sad, frustrated, annoyed, irritated, insecure, embarrassed, or angry? If you're anything like the typical human being, you find yourself choosing problematic behaviors and responses.

- You shut down, avoid, withdraw, isolate, or give the cold shoulder.

- You get defensive, avoid taking responsibility, and become quick to blame others.

- You erupt in aggressive behavior, yelling, screaming or even using physical aggression such as hitting or punching something.

- You gossip, demean, cut other people down, or harshly criticize those around you.

- You escape by defaulting to unhealthy ways of coping like shopping, drinking, binge eating, binge-watching, or any other addictive tendencies you keep close by.

- You _____. I left this one blank, just for you. What ends up being the typical consequence in your life? Is there something that just keeps happening again and again that seems to cause more harm than good?

If you stop to think about it, you'll likely find that same pattern playing out in your own life. But here's what I find most hopeful: the next letter is D. Sure, I've added that one on myself, but it's only because I believe it with all my heart: D stands for *do it differently.*

Our brains are really good at taking the path of least resistance.

DO IT DIFFERENTLY

By God's grace, you're not stuck to a pattern of dysfunction or unhealthy interactions. You have the power to do it differently. To change. To try something new. You don't have to keep going back to your default mode again and again and again. In fact, because of God at work in your life, you have the power to take hold of those pesky little thoughts and replace them with truth. Romans 12:2 calls it *renewing your mind*, and the promise is that it will lead to transformation! And transformed thoughts will lead to transformed feelings, which will lead to a transformed life. *Don't follow the patterns of this world. Do things differently.*

We're going to do some deeper work on your thought life, I promise—but for now I want to leave you with the hope that you don't have to keep doing the same things again and again. In fact, you've got to *do it differently.* When we start to recognize the thoughts, feelings, and behaviors we typically default to, we can begin to choose a different path. Change is as possible, as real, and as close as A-B-C-D.

I want you to know that I believe in you. God believes in you. You have what it takes to choose a new path for your life. No matter what your default mode has been in the past, no matter what default actions and reactions have been passed down to you, you can choose to do it differently.

VERSE FOR REFLECTION

"Do not conform to the pattern of this world, but be transformed by the renewing of your mind. Then you will be able to test and approve what God's will is—his good, pleasing and perfect will" (Romans 12:2).

TODAY'S HABIT: DO IT DIFFERENTLY

1. Let's talk about the ABCs in your life. Is there an activating event (A) that tends to be your biggest problem spot? If you can't think of one that happens again and again, write down one from this past month.

2. What were the flurry of negative thoughts and beliefs (B) that came with that activating event?

3. What consequences (C)—negative feelings and behaviors— came from those beliefs?

4. What is the default reaction you tend to have to negative emotions? (See the list above for ideas, and then come up with your own.) What is the default mode you've seen in your family of origin?

5. I want you to imagine yourself doing it differently. What does that look like? Write out a scenario with an activating event followed by beliefs and consequences—but this time, write how you would like to see yourself do it differently. What does a healthy version of the ABCs look like for you?

9

WHAT'S ON REPLAY?

OWN YOUR THOUGHTS

Have you ever had one of those moments when you're driving somewhere—to church, or the gym, or a friend's house—and all of a sudden you find yourself driving to work or another familiar place? Your mind is so accustomed to taking you to another place every single day that it ends up saving that route in your mental factory setting. Your mind loves to do the same things over and over again because patterns take less energy. Again, the brain loves the path of least resistance. Because of that, when you're not deliberately leading your mind on a different path—paying attention to the directions and being intentional about where you're going—you end up just following along with what your mind is used to doing...and you end up in the wrong place.

The same thing goes with our thought life. We have a tendency to *follow* our thoughts instead of *leading* our thoughts, because, honestly, it's just easier. And because our default thought processing happens so naturally, so automatically, it takes deliberation and intentionality to take ownership of our thoughts and make sure we're thinking in a healthy way.

What creates our default thought process? Well, to put it simply, our past experiences. The events that we've lived through, the responses and behaviors we've seen modeled, and repeated exposure to circumstances all play a primary role in how we think in the present. For most of us, the biggest factor in our default thought process is our family of origin—the way we grew up, the family we grew up in, and the way they interacted with us. We learn so much about life based on how life was modeled to us from a young age. So much of what we think and believe about ourselves and about life comes from our default patterns of thinking that we develop from childhood. For example, take the thought, *I have to be good in order to be loved.* Unintentionally, these harmful and untrue beliefs get integrated into our thought lives as well as our interactions with others. Over the many years I've worked with clients in my counseling office, here are some of the default thoughts people have shared with me:

- *You have to work hard in order to be valuable.* (Maybe this came from a work-ethic-focused family where affection was given in exchange for productivity.)

- *People will not stick around if I don't give them a reason to stay.* (Maybe this came from a child who was abandoned by a parent, or who was "left" as a result of divorce or other traumatic experience.)

- *I have to care for others and not myself.* (Maybe this came from a family where the parents were more concerned about their needs than the child's.)

- *Showing my true feelings is a sign of weakness.* (Maybe this came from a situation where feelings were dismissed or viewed in a negative light.)

- *I just don't fit in and I never will.* (Maybe this came from an experience of feeling left out or unwanted.)

- *I'm just better than everyone else.* (Maybe this came from a home lacking in healthy correction and discipline.)

- *Life is dangerous and bad things will happen.* (Maybe this came from traumatic experiences or a lack of feeling protected and safe.)

These responses give you an idea of some of the ways our minds create a default template to think and process from. And hopefully you're starting to understand why these types of thinking patterns can be dangerous in our lives. Because if *I have to be good in order to be loved,* I'm going to spend the rest of my life trying to be good, and moral, and do everything perfectly. And when I can't? I'll find myself down, depressed, feeling unworthy of love. These deep-seated beliefs motivate our behaviors and reactions. They will start to own us unless we begin to own them.

DEFAULT MODE

Hannah was battling negative thinking without even being aware of it. All she knew was that she felt pretty bad about herself more often than not. She battled feelings of guilt, depression, and insecurity. She often felt left out in her family, with her friends, and sometimes, even in her marriage.

When I started working with Hannah, I asked her to take a few moments, right in the middle of our counseling session, to try to figure out some of the underlying or default thoughts that were fueling her feelings of inadequacy. "I'm not really sure," she said right away.

I encouraged her to stay with it: "It's okay not to know right away, because sometimes the thoughts are so familiar we don't even recognize them. But let's take a few minutes to tune in, and then we'll talk through it."

She thought for a moment, and said, "I guess I think that I'm the problem. Something is wrong with me. I'm always wondering if there's something that I need to do or to change in order to make people like me."

A genuine sigh of empathy released from my lips, and I asked, "How long have you wondered those things?"

"I guess…my whole life. If I'm honest, as far back as I remember." We found ourselves talking through her default mode of thinking and getting to the roots, which actually went back to the early years of her adoption. "I remember telling you in one of our first sessions," Hannah said, "that I truly believe being adopted didn't have a negative effect on me, since I was adopted into such a wonderful, loving family. But as we're talking through this now, I can't help but wonder if some of those thoughts of not being wanted, feeling left out and inadequate, have to do with those early experiences. Deep down, I've always wondered where I really belong. I wonder if I've carried some of that default thinking into my own marriage, into how I parent my kids, and even into my interactions with my friends."

Hannah was starting to make the connections. This cycle of struggle had an underlying reason. It was being fueled by a pattern of negative and unhealthy default thinking that had been quietly humming in the background of her life, without her awareness.

After our session was over, I asked Hannah to tune into her default mode. I gave her an assignment to keep track of her thoughts over the next 24 hours. Every time a specific negative thought popped into her mind, she would jot it down in her phone or in a little notebook she kept in her pocket. If she wanted to change her default negative thinking, she had to recognize it first.

If you want to change your default thinking,
you have to recognize it first.

OWN THEM BEFORE THEY OWN YOU

Second Corinthians 10:5 admonishes us, "Take captive every thought to make it obedient to Christ." *Catch your thoughts.* Recognize them. Grab them before they get out there and take control. Own them before they own you. A huge part of being a mentally and emotionally healthy person is to get in the habit of facing your thoughts, but even deeper, to get to the root of why you have those thoughts to begin with. Where did that thought process come from? How did it become a part of your life?

If thoughts lead to feelings which lead to behaviors, this is where real change begins. It takes intention to recognize the thoughts that are on replay in your mind and change the playlist to something better, something healthier, something true.

Let's spend some time today working on recognizing your default ways of thinking and replacing them with truth. But remember, this isn't a once-and-done process. It took years to develop your current mental playlist of thoughts, so expect that it will take some time and energy to create a new playlist. But little by little, one thought at a time, this new way of thinking will become the norm. You'll learn to change your default. Before you know it, you'll own your thoughts before they own you.

VERSE FOR REFLECTION

"We take captive every thought to make it obedient to Christ" (2 Corinthians 10:5).

TODAY'S HABIT: OWN YOUR THOUGHTS

1. Take a small notebook with you today or pull up the notes app on your phone and write the heading "Default Thinking" at the top.

2. For the next 24 hours, write down any negative thoughts that pop into your mind about anything and everything, and especially if they have to do with yourself. We'll look a little deeper into those thoughts in the coming day.

10

THERE IT IS AGAIN

LOOK FOR PATTERNS

Have you ever heard a new phrase, song, or saying for the first time ever, and somehow over the course of the next few days or weeks you start hearing it everywhere? Or maybe you notice a sleek red car drive by that you've never seen before, and then you start seeing it in every parking lot. Or maybe you learn about a style of house while you're watching HGTV, and next thing you know you spot it all over your city or town. Could there really be an increase of people buying that sleek red car you noticed, or that new style of house? Or are you just more aware of it now?

This is a concept we refer to in psychology as *frequency bias,* and it can happen with pretty much anything. The fancy name for this is the Baader-Meinhof phenomenon. And if you've never heard of it before, there's a good chance you will after today. (See what I did there?) The main idea is that the frequency of those things is not actually increasing, but simply your awareness of them. And that awareness changes everything.

There's so much going on around you in one particular 24-hour period that it's impossible for your brain to absorb it all. But when you bring your attention to something—which is called selective attention—you begin to make note of that specific thing more and more often. Your brain tunes into it!

LOOKING FOR PATTERNS

What if we could begin to apply this frequency bias to our thoughts? What if we could increase our awareness and start to see and understand our thoughts in ways we didn't before? What if we could actually tune in to our patterns of thinking rather than just defaulting to our usual? The incredible thing is, we can.

In the last daily practice, I asked you to write down all the negative thoughts you had in a 24-hour period. If you haven't had a chance to do that, I want you to stop, go back to the practice before, and spend some time there first; we need to have something to work with if we want to identify patterns. Now, I want you to take a look at the thoughts you wrote down.

Do any patterns emerge?

Are there any themes that you tend to default to again, and again, and again?

Let's try to isolate those today. We're trying to get to the root of why you think the way you do. And to do that, we need to see if we can find some patterns.

God gives us permission to change the pattern. We have the power and control to *choose* which thoughts we will tune into and ruminate on throughout the day. So much of the Bible aligns with healthy psychology and counseling. God knows our tendency to default to the negative, so we're being asked to make it a habit, a daily practice, to tune in to whatever is good, pure, true, lovely (Philippians 4:8). We're being challenged to increase our awareness of the right thoughts and beliefs throughout the day and throughout our lives. *Don't just default to your usual, mindless patterns. Change the patterns.* But to do that, we've got to first stop and take note of our patterns—both the good and the bad— so we can begin to change the way we think. We have to recognize our patterns if we want to replace our patterns. And when we do that, it will begin to change everything. Because thought change leads to life change.

When Hannah, from the last lesson, wrote down all the negative thoughts she had in a day, she came in with a list longer than she'd expected. Here's what it read:

I don't fit in.

They're just pretending to like me.

He's just being nice because he feels sorry for me.

I can't believe I yelled at the kids. I am the worst mom.

If I don't get it together, he's going to leave me.

They invited me out of pity, but they don't really want me there.

I don't have what it takes to get it done today.

And those were just some of the things she had on her list. When she actually faced her thoughts, she realized how consistently mean, degrading, negative, and unhealthy they were. When I asked her to see if she could find a pattern, she realized she was stuck in a spiral of thoughts with a theme of inadequacy. She was never good enough—not in her personal life, not in her marriage, not in her friendships, not as a mom, or a homemaker, or a businesswoman. Her thoughts were always pointing out where she wasn't measuring up, fixating on all that was lacking. Now that she recognized a theme to her negative thinking, she started seeing it in almost every aspect of her life.

We have to recognize our patterns
if we want to replace our patterns.

CONNECTING THE DOTS

Why was Hannah caught in a cycle of toxic thinking? Why did she always feel like she wasn't enough? Long ago, Hannah started defaulting to this way of thinking to try to make sense of why she was adopted. This wasn't a conscious decision on her part—she was so young at the time. But sometimes our brains process things *for us*, without our permission or awareness. The brain tries to make sense of the world around us, and its interpretation may or may not be based on truth.

Young Hannah's mind needed to make sense of the fact that her biological parents had given her up for adoption. It was less painful for her to believe that she was the problem than it was for her to believe that something went terribly wrong with her biological parents. *There must have been something they didn't like about me. There must have been something wrong with me. I must not have been what they wanted. I must not be good enough.* This is where the seeds of her default thinking were planted—watered by the circumstances of life, fertilized by more unhealthy thinking, until she grew up learning to believe those thoughts and apply them to other areas of her life. They had become a part of her thought process without her awareness.

For Hannah to be freed from her default thinking, she needed a reset. She began by recognizing her negative thoughts, but that alone wasn't enough. Now she actually had to replace them with truth.

In your life, too, it isn't enough to simply stop thinking negative thoughts. You have to go the next step and begin thinking truthful thoughts. Replace them with truth, over and over again, until something begins to change—until *you* begin to change.

Debra, are you saying that if I just think healthy thoughts enough, I'll actually start believing them? That's exactly what I'm saying. It took you many years to build up your default thinking, so don't expect things to change overnight. But when you begin to fill your mind with truth, you also fill your *life* with truth. Things begin to change.

It may not seem like you're doing much—repeating positive statements of truth instead of your negative default thinking—but when you begin replacing your negative thinking with truth, you're changing the function of your brain. Every thought you think releases some sort of neurochemical. Negative thoughts release stress chemicals, and positive ones release feel-good chemicals. So, when you change your thoughts, you *literally* change your brain. Your brain is neuroplastic, which means it's malleable—it can change. You have the power to change how your brain works, and in turn how you feel and what you do, just by changing your thoughts.

God made our brains, and He knows best the value and importance of thinking about whatever is true, and noble, and right, and pure, and lovely, and admirable. Philippians 4:8 is not just a sweet, sentimental verse in the Bible—it's life or death. Your thoughts have the power to seriously enhance or completely destroy your life. If you see the same stream of thinking coming back again, and again, and again, it's time to own up to it and let the mental battle begin. Change your thought patterns, and you'll change your life patterns.

VERSE FOR REFLECTION

"Whatever is true, whatever is noble, whatever is right, whatever is pure, whatever is lovely, whatever is admirable—if anything is excellent or praiseworthy—think about such things" (Philippians 4:8).

TODAY'S HABIT: LOOK FOR PATTERNS

1. Holding your thoughts from the last 24 hours in front of you, look for patterns by asking yourself some of these questions:

   Do your negative thoughts tend to center around a theme, such as believing that you're unloved, uncapable, unworthy, unaccepted, or unappreciated?

   Do your thoughts reinforce the negative beliefs that you are powerless, insecure, weak, blemished, or alone?

   Do your thoughts involve worst-case scenarios, fears, and doubts?

   Do your negative thoughts tend to focus in on yourself, on others, or on God?

2. Write down any patterns in your thinking that you've observed. If you're having a hard time finding patterns, keep track of your thoughts for another 24-hour period. (You may even have to do this a few times before you start seeing themes emerge.) We'll talk in more detail about patterns in the next daily practice.

3. Spend some time in prayer, asking God for help in recognizing your default negative patterns, and then replacing them with God's truth—whatever is true, noble, right, pure, lovely, admirable, excellent, or praiseworthy.

4. On one side of a piece of paper, write out the top five negative thoughts or themes that seem to come up again and again. On the other side, write out something true, noble, right, pure, lovely, admirable, excellent, or praiseworthy to replace the negative default thinking with positive truthful thinking. God's Word is always a great place to look for truthful thoughts. Read through the positive list out loud five times, focusing on each one as you read. Repeat this activity on a weekly or daily basis, as needed, until you notice your negative thinking begin to shift and change.

Suggestions for Truthful Thinking Based on God's Word

I am chosen by God. (1 Peter 2:9)

I am forgiven of my sins. (Ephesians 1:7)

I am created to do the good work God has called me to do. (Ephesians 2:10)

I am made new in Christ. (2 Corinthians 5:17)

I can do what I need to do to thrive in this life through Christ who gives me strength. (Philippians 4:13)

God will take care of all my needs. (Philippians 4:19)

I have the power of the Holy Spirit. (Mark 16:17-18)

I have access to the peace of God which surpasses understanding. (Philippians 4:7)

I am born of God and able to conquer sin. (1 John 5:18)

God has given me everything I need to live a godly life. (2 Peter 1:3-4)

My body is a temple of the Holy Spirit. (1 Corinthians 6:19)

God has delivered me from darkness. (Colossians 1:13)

I am healed through Christ. (Isaiah 53:5)

I am loved by God. (Ephesians 2:4)

I am not ruled by fear. (2 Timothy 1:7)

Take some time to search God's Word for specific truths to battle your negative thinking.

CALL OUT THE LIES

RECOGNIZE COGNITIVE DISTORTIONS

S ome people are what we call *pathological liars*. They lie about everything. We don't exactly know why they do it—perhaps they lie out of fear, or because they're trying to avoid pain, or because of past trauma. But we know this: Lying is their one and only coping mechanism, and it's usually rooted in some form of mental illness. They lie to get what they want. They lie regardless of whether it hurts the people around them. They lie whether they feel like it's necessary or unnecessary. It becomes a part of the way they live. They lie so much that they begin to believe their own lies, and eventually they have a hard time separating the lies from reality. Ultimately, they end up living in a false sense of reality, and they bring the people around them into their web of lies.

It can be easy to fall for these lies because dangerous lies are subtle. Dangerous lies have just a tiny bit of truth in them, so they can begin to distort your thinking and make you doubt what you thought you knew. Dangerous lies make you question your own reality and default to the reality of the stronger, more convincing personality.

Let me clue you in on something you may have forgotten: Satan is a pathological liar. He comes as the father of lies (John 8:44), doing whatever he can to pull you from God's truth and bring you into his false reality, in which you are powerless, unloved, unwanted, unworthy, and far away from God. But these lies can be so subtle that we hardly even notice them. In counseling and psychology, we call these subtle lies *cognitive distortions*. So many of us are battling these lies right here and right now, with or without our awareness. The struggle is real. The battle is on.

In short, a cognitive distortion is an inaccurate or warped lens through which we see the world. It's like picking up a pair of cracked, foggy, smudged glasses that aren't even the right prescription and using them to navigate through life. You can see just enough to make you think what you're seeing is correct. Just a tiny bit of truth. But a tiny bit of truth laced with a massive amount of lies still adds up to a lie. The interesting thing about a pair of dirty glasses is that after a while you get so used to the dirt that you learn to see through it. The dirt becomes so familiar that you even forget it's there. And we have a tendency to keep choosing what's familiar over what's healthy—until someone calls us out.

It's time to take a good hard look at the cognitive distortions that tend to cloud your judgment and fog your perspective.

You've got your own distorted glasses on. That's me, calling you out. But we all have those glasses because we've all been through hard things, hurts, trauma, and pain. We've been let down, rejected, and shamed. We've been used, abused, and neglected. And all those hard things begin to add cracks, smudges, and smears to our lenses. They begin to affect how we see ourselves and how we see the world. Let me share some of the most common cognitive distortions with you.[1]

Black-and-white thinking/All-or-nothing thinking: The tendency to see things in extremes rather than having a balanced perspective.

Overgeneralization: The tendency to take one negative experience or interaction and unfairly apply it to other situations.

Minimization and magnification: The tendency to make little of the good things and make much of the bad things.

Mind reading: The tendency to assume that others are thinking or feeling something negative toward you.

Fortune-telling: The tendency to predict the future and imagine negative outcomes.

Catastrophizing: The tendency to think in worst-case scenarios.

Emotional reasoning: The tendency to believe everything your emotions tell you. (Remember, emotions are real, but they aren't always telling the truth!)

Could-should-would: The tendency to fixate on the past with regret, rehearsing what you could have, should have, or would have done differently.

Labeling: The tendency to use broad names or stereotypes to identify yourself or others in a negative way.

Personalization: The tendency to take the actions and interactions of others very personally rather than see them objectively.

As you read through the list above, ask yourself which lies have you been believing. Which of the false lenses above have you been wearing as you look out at the world and the people around you? It's time to take a good hard look at the cognitive distortions that tend to cloud your judgment and fog your perspective. It's time to recognize the lies that have been holding you back and keeping you stuck.

VERSE FOR REFLECTION

"[The devil] is a liar and the father of lies" (John 8:44).

TODAY'S HABIT: RECOGNIZE COGNITIVE DISTORTIONS

1. Which of the cognitive distortions do you tend to struggle with? Pick three that you relate to the most.

2. Write some specific examples of ways you have used that cognitive distortion to interpret life. As you write, try to identify the subtle truth in that lie, and distinguish it from the lie you might be believing.

3. Look for those three specific cognitive distortions in how you act, think, and interact throughout the rest of today or throughout your day tomorrow. Hint, many times you can see them most clearly in how you interact with others.

12

CHOOSING A SIDE

SHIFT YOUR STORY

E very story has two sides.

Google "optical illusion, what do you see?" sometime today, and you'll get a series of pictures that can be seen in two different ways. One of the most famous is a black-and-white image where you either see the silhouettes of two men or a fancy candlestick. In another one, you either see the silhouette of a young girl or the wrinkled face of an old one. If you've never seen these images before you're probably so confused right now; the options I'm listing are so extremely different from one another. How can you either see two men or a candlestick? And isn't an old woman very different in appearance from a young girl? It all depends on what you focus on. What you allow your eyes to fixate on is the picture that will emerge from the image. It's an optical illusion, but it's also a fine illustration for life.

In our lives as well, there are two sides to every story. It's all a matter of what we choose to focus on. Take for example my personal perspective on the past few years:

PERSPECTIVE 1

The year 2020 marked a new era for so many people, myself included. It was an era filled with fear, uncertainty, and the unknown.

COVID-19 was introduced to our world, and we lost control of the lives we thought we knew. From lockdowns to quarantine to social distancing, we lost our ability to connect and communicate with one another. There were times when I couldn't hug my parents, spend face-to-face time with my friends, or even go to church and worship the way I wanted. Isolation became a part of our culture. Danger and death seemed to lurk everywhere. I said heart-wrenching good-byes to friends and family members whose lives were taken by this deadly disease. My children are growing up in a world marked by instability and uncertainty. We have no idea what tomorrow holds, or if things will ever change. The past few years have been some of the hardest we've ever walked through, and sadly, there seems to be no end in sight.

PERSPECTIVE 2

The year 2020 marked a new era for so many people, myself included. It was an era filled with more opportunities than ever to cling to the Lord and trust Him with the uncertainty of tomorrow. When COVID-19 was introduced to our world, we had to drop the illusion of control. It's freeing to know that we're not in control, but God is. From lockdowns to quarantine to social distancing, we leaned into the gift of modern technology, and we got to FaceTime, Zoom, and video chat with our loved ones even when times were tough. What a gift it was to connect like this, when we couldn't be together face-to-face. There were times when I laughed with my parents over Face-Time, had Zoom "dinner dates" with friends, or even got to stream in and watch my church service online, worshiping with others no matter what was going on in the world around us. We realized how much we needed one another, and we learned to share that love in a way we never had before. Hope and life grew even in the darkest places. My husband and I ended up getting unexpectedly pregnant in the middle of 2020 (thanks to a little boredom and a whole lot of lockdown!) and we welcomed our beautiful, miraculous, surprise rainbow baby, Ethan. He was such a joy in these unexpected times. I said heart-wrenching goodbyes to friends and family members who were called to heaven during this hard time. But what a reminder that this world is not our home! We were able to grieve with the true hope of heaven, being reminded to live life to the fullest while we have it. My children now have to grow up in a world where each day is literally an act of trusting God for today. We have no idea what tomorrow holds, but God holds our tomorrow. In that, we can have a peace that passes our understanding. A peace that floods us in the hard moments. The past few years have been some of the hardest we've ever walked through, but thankfully, we've never had to walk alone. God's presence in our lives has been nearer than ever before. But maybe because we've been looking for it in ways we never have before. And that is a true gift.

• • •

My friend, there are two sides to *every* story. Every single one. Your story included. And how we tell ourselves the story is going to have a huge effect on how we live out the story. There are two options set before us: to focus on the good or focus on the bad. To choose the right road, or to choose the wrong road. To fixate on what we have or ruminate on what we don't have. And we get to choose which perspective we live out of. Each and every single day.

That's not to say we ignore, repress, or make light of the hard things—no, we have to acknowledge them, face them, and deal with them—but we can't stay there. We can't get stuck. We can't allow those things to define the story. Because that is neither accurate nor healthy. So, I ask you this: Which side of the story will you choose to focus on today?

How we tell ourselves the story has a
huge effect on how we live it out.

VERSE FOR REFLECTION

"A wise person chooses the right road; a fool takes the wrong road" (Ecclesiastes 10:2 NLT).

TODAY'S HABIT: SHIFT YOUR STORY

1. There are two sides to your story as well. Take some time today to write out a story from your past or present that has typically brought stress, frustration, fear, worry, shame, or some other difficult emotion. Write it out including all the hard things, just as I did in Perspective 1.

2. Now rewrite the story using a different perspective, as I did in Perspective 2. Make a point to highlight the positive things, areas of growth, the lessons learned, or opportunities that have come as a result.

3. Which side of the story do you tend to live out of?

13

WE GO WAY BACK

GO BACK TO GO FORWARD

To move forward, we have to first go backward. I know that may not be the typical message you hear in Sunday school. Many times, we want to do a quick brush over the past and focus on the present and the future.

The apostle Paul wrote, "Forgetting what is behind and straining toward what is ahead, I press on toward the goal to win the prize for which God has called me heavenward in Christ Jesus" (Philippians 3:13-14). We often misinterpret this to mean that you should literally "forget" your past. Forget the trauma, forget the pain, forget the hurts, forget the abuse, forget the betrayal, forget the abandonment, forget it all.

But please hear me on this: That's not what Paul is advising! Paul wasn't talking about forgetting his past *struggles*; he was talking about forgetting his past *victories*. He wasn't talking about forgetting his past *pain*; he was talking about forgetting his *pride* and his boasting in his accomplishments. Just a few verses earlier, he listed all the things he could boast in—all his victories and accomplishments: his accolades, statuses, and successes. What he's trying to say here is that his past identities are nothing compared to his identity in Christ!

Don't take this verse out of context and use it as an excuse to avoid looking back. To avoid grieving. To avoiding healing. Friend, let me remind you of a powerful reality: You have to deal with your past to be freed from your past! In fact, there could be some things in your past that are actually keeping you stuck today. Our emotional responses in the present are often rooted in our emotional wounds from the past.

If you were to come see me in my office for a counseling session, the first thing I would have you do is tell me about what's going on in the present. *What is the key issue that brought you in today?* We would discuss that issue at length and look for immediate solutions and practical next steps. You have to deal with alleviating the pain in the present, the most pressing symptoms first. It's like emergency room triage. If you come in with severe pain in your abdomen, we're going to help alleviate the pain first and foremost. But after that, we need to get to the root of what's causing this pain to begin with. It could be anything from indigestion to your appendix, all the way to pregnancy!

The same thing goes with emotional health: We need to get to the root. So as we continued your therapy process, eventually we would get to your past. Somewhere between sessions 2 and 6, I'd ask you to do what I call the Timeline Activity. I would ask you to write down significant events, starting from your earliest memories all the way to who you are today, and note experiences that have shaped you for both good and bad. And then we'd talk through it with our eyes open to themes that might come up again and again in your life. We're looking for emotional responses that might come up repeatedly without your awareness. We're looking for patterns. We're identifying roots.

Carla was one of those clients. She was so desperately trying to keep the relationships in her life strong that she was starting to feel exhausted, drained, and empty. She had a pattern of doing all or most of the work in her relationships—the giving, the serving, the forgiving, the initiating—out of fear that people wouldn't like her or wouldn't stick around. She felt like she had to prove to others that she was worth having around; she needed to be needed in order to feel secure in the relationship. But ultimately, she felt alone. She was trapped in a host of one-sided relationships, and her deepest fear of feeling alone was starting to become a reality.

When Carla engaged in the Timeline Activity, a very interesting theme started to emerge: the fear of abandonment. One of her very first significant memories was when Carla's mom and dad got a divorce, and shortly after, her mom walked out on the family. She didn't get an explanation—she just knew that she and her dad were on their own. Dad had never been much of the emotional or relational type, so it was up to Carla, the eldest daughter, to hold the family together.

Another experience she noted in her timeline was dating her first boyfriend in college. He was the captain of the football team, and she felt lucky that he even noticed her. The problem was that he wasn't invested in the relationship. She quickly felt the desperation to make sure he stayed, to make sure he realized how much he needed her in his life. She ended up doing everything she could to keep him close—giving, serving, forgiving, initiating—and then getting up and doing it all over again. Eventually, he broke up with her. Carla was devastated.

Again and again, in different stages of her life, we began noticing that pattern. Out of fear of abandonment, Carla ended up giving too much in the relationships around her. Out of a deep insecurity that a person would leave, she desperately gave everything she had. Even to people who didn't deserve it. Even to people who were too unhealthy to give back. As the pattern emerged, Carla opened her eyes to the fact that she had been functioning out of deep wounds for many years. These deep wounds caused patterns that started in early childhood but repeated themselves in different seasons of her life. Before she could begin to heal, she first needed to acknowledge the pain of being abandoned by her mom.

Your patterns might not be as obvious as Carla's, but let me assure you, they are there. Patterns emerge in how you act, interact, feel, think, or behave. Those patterns need to be called out, examined, and faced. Because the only way we can successfully move forward is when we have successfully looked back. We all go waaaaay back, my friends. And sometimes it takes going backward to move forward. You've got to face it to replace it. So let's go there. Let's do this. Together.

You've got to face it to replace it.

VERSE FOR REFLECTION

"Forgetting what is behind and straining toward what is ahead, I press on toward the goal to win the prize for which God has called me heavenward in Christ Jesus" (Philippians 3:13-14).

TODAY'S HABIT: GO BACK TO GO FORWARD

---

1. Timeline Activity: Write down significant life events, starting from your earliest memories all the way to today's events. Note the experiences that have shaped you for both good and bad.

2. Take the time to look through each event, specifically focusing on the difficult or hard events, and try to identify any patterns. Ask God to reveal something new to you today.

   Is there an emotional response you tend to have to yourself or others?

Is there an unhealthy belief you tend to hold on to that might have emerged from some of those experiences?

Is there a pattern to the way you do relationships (or to the way you avoid relationships)?

Is there a past wound (betrayal, abandonment, rejection, fear, neglect, apathy, abuse, control, judgment) that you've never allowed yourself to grieve and heal from?

How might that past emotional wound be affecting your life and decisions today?

3. If you're having a hard time finding patterns, or if you're real-izing there are unhealed wounds from the past or present

that you've never fully dealt with, consider working with a professional counselor to help you on this journey of healing. Learn more in Appendix B of this book, and visit www.DebraFileta.com/counseling for counseling resources and the opportunity to connect with me and my team at the Debra Fileta Counselors Network.

14

LIKE A CHILD

HEAL FROM CHILDHOOD WOUNDS

f I had to use one word to describe Brett when I met him, that word would be *stuck*. He was stuck in his relationships, stuck in his career, and stuck in his faith. He felt like he was spinning his wheels and getting nowhere. And in a way, he was right. He felt paralyzed when it came to making decisions in his life, unable to follow through with the change he wanted to see. He wanted his relationships to be better, but he couldn't seem to make that happen. He wanted a new job, but he couldn't seem to take the necessary steps to get there. He wanted his relationship with God to grow stronger, but he found himself falling back into apathy. "I don't know why I'm so stuck. I'm starting to wonder if I'm going to be stuck forever," he said to me, with hopeless tears filling his eyes.

I wanted to help Brett get unstuck. And to do that, we had to go backward before we could move forward. Just like I asked you to do in the last chapter, I asked Brett to complete a timeline so we could talk through significant experiences from his past and look for patterns we could apply to his present situation.

As Brett shared stories from his childhood, he admitted, "I haven't thought about these things in forever." Stories of getting bullied began to emerge, one after the other. Getting harassed and abused by his peers was part of his daily routine. The names they would hurl at him, the nasty jokes at his expense, the crude words that stung like nothing else could…Brett hung his head in shame as he shared how awful he felt each day, wanting so badly to blend in and not stick out so that maybe, just maybe, he wouldn't be noticed and avoid getting beat up and humiliated. As he shared, I helped him realize that he had been conditioned to be as quiet, as little, as passive, and as compliant as possible so no attention would come his way. He had been robbed of his confidence, his autonomy, his desire to be seen, noticed, and valued. "In a way," Brett said, "I carried that same mentality into my everyday life, trying not to stand out anywhere I went, including with my family, my friends, and even in my romantic life. I'm still compliant. Still passive. Still quiet. It's almost like I'm a little kid, just waiting for someone to tell me what to do, having no power of my own."

With that sentence, Brett started to make connections. He was stuck in the wounds of the past, living out of his 13-year-old self rather than the grown man he was here and now. Whenever it was time to make a decision, assert a need, or choose a path, that scared, insecure, compliant 13-year-old boy would emerge and get in the way of his confidence and his ability to act. How could he begin to break free from that pattern? How could he let go of his childhood responses and live with confidence, freedom, and autonomy?

When we get stuck in our wounds from childhood, we end up living out of a place of pain rather than a place of power.

CHILDHOOD SELF

There's a little child living inside each one of us. It's our childhood self. Without our awareness and without our permission, we can behave or react in ways that reflect that little child instead of living as the confident, secure, loved men and women of God we are. When we get stuck in our wounds from childhood, we end up living out of a place of pain rather than a place of power.

I want you to think about your childhood self for a moment. What were you like? What did you go through? How did you feel? Imagine yourself in the most vulnerable position you were in as a child. Maybe it was the pain and loneliness of your parents getting a divorce; maybe it was the worry and fears that plagued you because so many things were out of your control; maybe it was the deep sorrow you felt after losing a loved one; the dark shame you experienced after abuse; the unrelenting pressure of feeling like you had to be the best. Whatever it was, there's a child still living inside of you who feels those things. And if the wounds from your childhood aren't resolved, just like Brett, you'll find yourself defaulting back to that little child instead of living out of a place of freedom.

I've counseled so many people who feel stuck, not even realizing that they're still functioning out of past pain, fears, and insecurities. But it makes sense, doesn't it? We can't expect a little child to carry the weight and responsibility of life the way we can expect an adult to. So how do we take back control?

LIKE A CHILD

Jesus has so much compassion for children. With all the important passages we read in Scripture of the words Jesus actually spoke, we can see He took the time to specifically address children. This is so significant because during that time in Middle Eastern culture, children weren't inherently seen as important parts of society. Their value was commonly placed on how much they could contribute to the family. As one writer puts it, "Sometimes children were loved and sometimes exploited, depending upon how they were perceived as benefiting the family. Roman law gave the father absolute power over his family—which extended to life and death. As late as AD 60 a son was put to death by the simple order of his father."[1] Scripture was completely revolutionary in calling children a gift and a reward; in seeing them as precious, valuable, worthy of compassion and love (Psalm 127:3). When the disciples tried to keep the children away from Jesus, He was grieved, and He responded, "Let the little children come to me, and do not hinder them, for the kingdom of heaven belongs to such as these" (Mark 19:14). No matter who they were or what they had been though, there was always room for children by the feet of Jesus.

Do I have permission to speak to your inner child for just a moment? I'm asking the adult version of you, reading this book, to step aside for a bit, and call out that little child inside of you. That little Kathleen. That little Michael. That little John, Sarah, Peter, Jenny, or Chris. Call out that little child by name; picture his or her image in your mind's eye. Braces, pimples, mismatched clothing, awkward stance and all.

Now listen to me for a moment, little one: No matter what you've been through, how scared and alone you feel, how worried you might be about what's up ahead, how hurt you've been by mean people, how insecure you feel about who you are or what you have to offer the world, how much pressure you feel is on your shoulders right now, how out of control and scary your world seems to be, there's a place for you at the feet of Jesus. For you. *A place just for you.* He looks right at you with love, compassion, confidence, approval, and grace, and He wants you to begin to look at yourself the same way. No matter what you've been through, no matter what you feel about yourself, no matter what others have told you, no matter whether they've been there for you or not, Jesus is here for you. He always has been, and He always will be. He has given you everything you need to grow up into the strong, capable, secure, loving, kind, powerful, compassionate adult that He's made you to be. He believes in you, and He wants you to believe in yourself.

Can you speak those words over that little child within you? I sure hope so. I hope you speak those words again and again and again until you believe them. But I know that for some of you, that's hard. Rather than seeing that little child with compassion, care, kindness, and grace, you see them with bitterness, resentment, shame, and frustration. You wanted him to protect himself, to fight back, to be tougher. You wished she was stronger, wiser, prettier, or more competent. Maybe you've been spending your entire life trying to ignore or forget about that little child. Trying to become someone better.

My friend, Jesus loves you. He loves the adult version of you, the child version of you, and every bit in between. He looks on you with compassion and wants you to look at yourself the same way. You were a child. A little child. A child trying to do the best you could with what you had. Have grace with yourself. And realize that today, you are a strong, capable, kind person who has the power, freedom, and autonomy to choose a path for your life that moves you into a better place.

I always tell my clients that when dealing with our childhood selves, in a way, we have to "reparent" ourselves. We have to look at those childhood selves and help them find their way. God has given us all the power and perspective we need to live this life victoriously. So, every now and again, look that little child in the eyes with grace, compassion, and kindness, and remind them that they're okay, they're wanted, they're loved. But then remind them that they are no longer in control. They're off the hook. Their fear, shame, pain, insecurity, and anxiety cannot hold you back anymore. There's a place for them at the feet of Jesus. And there's a place for you too.

VERSE FOR REFLECTION

"Let the little children come to me, and do not hinder them, for the kingdom of heaven belongs to such as these" (Mark 19:14).

TODAY'S HABIT: HEAL FROM CHILDHOOD WOUNDS

1. As you consider your Timeline Activity, tune in to your child-hood self and the experiences you had growing up. What was your childhood self thinking, feeling, and experiencing?

2. Do you find that some of those same childhood thoughts, feelings, and experiences creep back into your life today? How so?

3. When you consider your childhood self, do you have an attitude of compassion, grace, and kindness? Or bitterness, resentment, and shame? Why?

4. What do you think your childhood self needs to hear from Jesus? What do you think your childhood self needs to hear from you?

5. How might unhealed wounds from your childhood be keeping you stuck today?

6. One practice I lead my clients in is addressing their childhood selves. Let me talk you through it using some of your answers from above:

  • Take a moment to focus in on one specific difficult moment in your childhood. Write down what you might have been thinking, feeling, and experiencing in that moment. Consider saying some of those things out loud—for example, "I was feeling abandoned, scared that I was alone, and worried that he would never come back."

  • Now I want you to consider this: What would Jesus say to your childhood self in that moment? What truths, words of compassion, or guidance would He offer to that little child? Write those things down.

  • Next, take a moment to speak those words of truth out loud over your childhood self. Take some time to pray and ask God to help you heal from some of those wounds from your past.

15

TOXIC OPTIMISM

FACE THE HARD STUFF

He cheated on me multiple times after ten years of marriage, and then left me for another woman," she said with a straight face, "but I know God works all things for good." It was our very first counseling session. She had just talked me through the awful details of the events leading up to this dark point in her life. But she told the whole story as if she were talking about someone else's life. Every disturbing detail, every difficult memory, was portrayed as if she was describing a movie she had watched rather than sharing the heart-wrenching details of her life. Her emotions were so detached from the situation that something felt off. To me, that was a red flag in and of itself.

It's easy to use spirituality to cover up our difficult emotions. It's easy to use theology or Christian-sounding platitudes to skip over our wounds, our hurts, and our pain.

> *There's a lot to be grateful for.*
>
> *So many people have gone through much worse.*
>
> *Everything happens for a reason.*
>
> *Time heals all wounds.*
>
> *It will all be okay in the end.*

You've probably heard some of these. You may have even said them to yourself or to someone else. A few chapters ago, we learned about the important practice of living out of a healthy perspective. But did you know that even a positive perspective can be taken too far if it's not grounded in reality? I don't want to confuse you, but I feel like if we're really going to practice being emotionally healthy people, we have to go here. We've got to talk about toxic optimism.

Toxic optimism is when we hide behind a positive perspective instead of truly dealing with the hard things. Just as it's not healthy to constantly live in a state of negative thinking or to fixate and ruminate on all the horrible things in life, it's also not healthy to pretend they don't exist. It's not healthy to cut off, dismiss, bypass, and repress the hard emotions of life and quickly brush them off with simple platitudes. In the name of optimism, or even in the name of "Christian spirituality," we end up preventing ourselves from healing. Real healing requires us to tend to the wound, and we can't do that well if we haven't acknowledged its severity. We can't tend to it if we're working hard to pretend it doesn't exist or trying to make ourselves believe it didn't hurt as bad as it did.

The adage "time heals all wounds" is one of my least favorite. Because time alone doesn't heal all wounds, and we can't pretend it does. In fact, when left with time, some wounds will only get more and more infected. They'll only get worse if they're ignored and not tended to. You can cover it up with a big Band-Aid and hope that it eventually goes away. But it's still there. And now it's even worse.

Our emotional wounds work much the same. And we often want to ignore them and hope that the passage of time, the pushing through, the Band-Aid of optimism and Christian-sounding platitudes will be the solution. But it's not. We need to *tend* to our emotional wounds. We need to recognize that they are real, they are painful, and they need our attention. It's vital to grieve the hard things. It's crucial to cry over the sad things. It's okay to get to the point where the wound is so painful you need to get some intervention—to see a therapist for counseling, or a doctor for medication, or a pastor for prayer, or all of the above. Pushing through with positivity is not the answer; it's actually a toxic response to the hard things. It's not only okay to feel hard things; it's important to allow yourself to feel them. Because God is in those too. He is with you on the mountaintop, and He is with you in the valley. He is near to the brokenhearted and those who feel crushed in spirit (Psalm 34:18). You don't have to have it all together and you don't have to put on your game face for Him to draw close. He is already here. And your wounds, pain, and difficult emotions don't scare Him. They draw Him near.

Jesus is clear: In this world you will have trouble (John 16:33). You are going to have wounds that need to be cared for. That's just a fact. The hope we have is that He has overcome this world! There will be an end to the trouble of this world—one day. There will be a solution to all our problems in this world—one day. There will be healing for every heartache and justice for every injustice in this world—because Christ has overcome all those things, and heaven is our eternal rest and peace for those of us who believe. But while we are in this world, we will have trouble. Let's not make light of that. Let's have respect for that. Let's have grace in that—for ourselves and for one another. And while we're here, let's make sure we acknowledge our hurts and tend to them in the best way we can.

Let's have the courage to face the hard things. Because the work of faith is not in the avoiding; the work of faith is in the facing.

We can't tend our wounds well if we
haven't acknowledged their severity.

VERSE FOR REFLECTION

"In this world you will have trouble. But take heart! I have overcome the world" (John 16:33).

TODAY'S HABIT: FACE THE HARD STUFF

1. Write down one hard circumstance from the past 12 months that you've been avoiding dealing with. What emotions, beliefs, or questions has it stirred up in you? What's one step you can take to face or confront them and begin to heal from that pain?

2. Is there an emotional wound, a pain point from your past or even from your present, that you've been afraid to face? Examples might include abuse from your childhood, a broken relationship, an addiction or unhealthy behavior in your life, ongoing conflict with a loved one, obstacles at work, or a traumatic event or experience. Write it down. Take some time to journal your thoughts, feelings, and reactions to that circumstance.

3. Take some time to pray about this specific situation and consider what the next step to "facing" this hard thing could look like. Perhaps:

    Confronting someone about the pain they've caused you.

    Pursuing a posture of empathy to understand the other person's perspective.

Finding a close friend or trusted mentor to share and talk about your pain.

Investing in a season of professional counseling to heal from that hard experience.

Setting boundaries to protect yourself and to prevent ongoing hurt.

Acknowledging your own frailty, limitations, or wrongdoing in the situation.

Practicing forgiveness toward the person who hurt you to free yourself from the pain.

What is the next step for you?

16

PRESSURE CHECK

ASSESS YOUR STRESS LEVELS

Human beings are like volcanos. Whether or not we're aware of it, there's always pressure building underneath the surface. The pressure of trying to stay afloat financially or even get out of debt. The pressure from conflict or tension in our marriage. The pressure of trying to raise children in a chaotic and ever-changing world. The pressure of dealing with an ailing parent. The pressure of trying to succeed in our job, career, or ministry. The pressure of dealing with the unforeseen stressors, new norms, and strong opinions of a post-Covid world. The pressure of navigating the racial and ethnic divides we're facing in our country. The pressure of trying to please, appease, and make peace with the people in our lives. The pressure of keeping up with the filters, fads, and friends in a social media-obsessed world. Pressure, pressure, pressure.

Slowly, the pressure begins to build. And when the pressure gets too high it needs to go somewhere. It needs to be released. Ultimately, if we don't deal with the pressure in a healthy way, it will find the point of least resistance. And just like a volcano, that pressure will burst through into our lives in an emotional explosion.

This emotional explosion looks different for different people. For many people, the emotional explosion happens through the surfacing of a mental health struggle such as depression, anxiety, or panic attacks—what some people refer to as a "mental breakdown."[1] For others, it comes in the form of relationship tension and conflict with the people closest to them. Maybe it comes in the form of uncontrolled emotions like anger, rage, or aggression. Maybe it comes in the form of suppressed emotions like apathy, withdrawal, and isolation. It could come as burnout and irritability; addictions or substance abuse; medical or health problems. But the idea is the same, and the signal is clear: There's something going on underneath the surface that needs to be dealt with. The pressure has been building, and it's time to recognize it and deal with it.

You can't be an emotionally healthy person if you don't stop to do a pressure check, to take time to search your heart and mind. Psalm 139:23-24 says, "Search me, O God, and know my heart! Try me and know my thoughts! And see if there be any grievous way in me, and lead me in the way everlasting" (esv). I love this passage because it reminds me to stop and search, to stop and look in, to stop and take inventory. To stop and ask: "What's happening underneath the surface? What pressures am I facing in my life today?" In fact, we can swap out the word *pressure* for the word *stress*: a buildup of mental or emotional strain and tension. We use that word a lot in our society. Everyone is "stressed" about something. The problem is, we don't often take the time to discern what, or how much stress we're really dealing with until it's too late. Until that pressure makes its way to the surface and causes more damage than we ever imagined it could.

Pressure checks shouldn't be a once-and-done experience. Maybe you did a pressure check a couple years ago. It's time to do it again. Because pressure builds and changes over different seasons of our lives, it's necessary to stop and check in on a regular basis—even if you don't feel the need to. Sometimes the pressure buildup is hard to notice.

One thing many people don't realize is that pressure can build up as a result of the hard situations we go through just as much as the good situations we go through. The good and the difficult in life both cause pressure. A baseline level of stress comes with any sort of change, even if it's a positive one.

We use a tool in counseling called the Holmes-Rahe Life Stress Inventory to help you assess your level of stress (which you'll use today as a part of your daily practice).[2] In fact, the Holmes-Rahe Life Stress Inventory can predict your likelihood of having an "emotional explosion" based on your levels of stress. The more change you've experienced in a condensed period of time, the more likely that the pressure is building underneath the surface. But what you'll notice right away in this stress inventory is that positive events are listed right alongside difficult ones—a vacation can cause about as much stress as getting a traffic ticket! Trouble with the in-laws can cause about the same amount of stress as an outstanding personal achievement! Change, in any form, brings with it a baseline level of stress.

On my *Love and Relationships* podcast, I started a series of on-air counseling sessions with some of the most notable Christian teachers and leaders of today, and called it the "Are You Really OK?" series. The goal of these sessions was to ask leaders how they're really doing, to open up and start conversations about mental and emotional health, and show people that no matter who we are, we're all susceptible to the struggle.

My very first on-air session was with a high-capacity pastor of a megachurch. At the height of his career, with an incredible new job offer pending, he found himself having a series of severe and debilitating panic attacks. But the thing is, he didn't know they were panic attacks at first. He truly thought he was having a heart attack. The pressure had gotten so bad that it was starting to affect his body. "I just kept putting things on my plate, and putting things on my plate, and putting things on my plate without scraping anything off." Eventually, the pressure got to a point where it affected his mental health in a serious way. Here's how he described what was going on in his mind during his first panic episode: "I thought: *I'm not going to walk my daughters down the aisle, I'm about to die on the side of this road at 36 years old of a heart attack. This is how I go out. This is the end.*"[3]

He had just finished speaking to a room of 25,000 people. Ministry was happening, people were responding, and life was full. But maybe a little *too* full. He was so busy navigating a season of good things that he didn't stop to do a pressure check and see how he was really doing underneath the surface. And eventually, it caught up to him.

Because here's the thing: even high-capacity people have a limited capacity. Our mental and emotional functions have a max. We *can* get to a place where we can't handle one more thing, so we have to regularly tune in to what's going on inside ourselves to make sure we don't get there. After all, you don't take your car to get a tune-up after it breaks down; you take it in before—for regular maintenance, oil changes, and tire rotations. Let's get ahead of the curve of our own emotional health. Let's stop for regular tune-ups, and check-ins, and pressure checks and make sure we don't get to the point of emotional explosion. Let's be mindful of our limited capacity and make sure we're taking steps to both limit the pressure and release it in a healthy way.

Let's get ahead of the curve of our own emotional health.

VERSE FOR REFLECTION

"Search me, O God, and know my heart! Try me and know my thoughts! And see if there be any grievous way in me, and lead me in the way everlasting!" (Psalm 139:23-24 ESV).

TODAY'S HABIT: ASSESS YOUR STRESS LEVELS

1. Go to www.DebraFileta.com/resources to download and print a copy of the Holmes-Rahe Life Stress Inventory. Fill it out, taking note of the pressure you've faced in the last 12 months and adding up your total points to find your score. Based on your score, this inventory will help determine your susceptibility to having a stress-induced health breakdown in the next two years. Take some time to do a pressure check.

2. Reflecting on your inventory score, are you surprised by your stress level? Is there anything else that might be adding stress to your life that wasn't mentioned on the inventory?

3. On a scale of one to ten (ten being the most pressure) how much pressure do you feel like you have in your life right now?

4. Consider one or two ways you can begin to alleviate this pressure in a healthy way as well as one or two ways you can begin to limit the pressure. We'll be discussing pressure release in detail and equipping you with practical steps in the next daily practice.

PRESSURE RELEASE

IDENTIFY YOUR COPING SKILLS

I saw a photo of a two-story house that had been completely obliterated. It was stripped down to its bare bones: The roof was totally gone, the outer brick and siding had been fully blown away, the windows had been blown out, and the shutters and doors were hanging by their hinges. Black soot, debris and glass, and broken pieces of wood were strewn everywhere. It looked like a bomb had exploded inside this home. And in a way, that's kind of what happened. Because what had actually caused the demolition of this house was a buildup of pressure from the water heater.

"A water heater explosion produces enough force to completely destroy your home," explains one contracting company. "Water heaters rely on both pressure and high temperatures. A water heater explosion often occurs when either (or both) of these factors reach dangerous levels that cannot be resolved through safety mechanisms like the temperature and pressure relief valve."[1] In this case, the pressure release valve was clogged. So, the pressure built up...and built up...and built up...and caused this massive explosion that destroyed the entire house.

In our last lesson, we talked about how each of us is like a volcano, and we've got to keep a check on our pressure. If you want to keep pressure from destroying you, you've got to have a pressure release valve.

We can do that by making sure we have healthy outlets for that pressure—deliberate and intentional ways to release the stress and cope with the pressure. In counseling, we call these our "coping skills."

If you want to keep pressure from destroying you,
you've got to have a pressure release valve.

Coping skills aren't just something you're born with; they're something you've got to learn. And we can learn unhealthy coping skills just as readily as we can learn healthy coping skills. But why don't you take a wild guess about which set is easier to learn? You got that right. The unhealthy ones. Because they're usually modeled to us in society and culture. They're the ones we may have learned from our parents, family members, or friends. Because they don't require much effort to engage in, unhealthy coping skills are easier to pick up by default.

When it comes to assessing your coping skills, here's the one and only question you need to ask yourself: *When I'm feeling stressed, what do I usually do to release that pressure?* Let's see which set of coping skills below you tend to default to.

EXAMPLES OF UNHEALTHY COPING SKILLS

- Mindless scrolling through social media.

- Zoning out in front of YouTube, Netflix, TV, news, or some other form of screen-induced distraction.

- Defaulting to eating unhealthy food, drinking alcohol, shopping, gambling, pornography—or any other addictive behavior.

- Procrastinating on an assignment, chore, or task.

- Sleeping too much or too little.

- Withdrawing from relationships, people, and activities.

- Interacting with people in an aggressive, passive-aggressive, or conflict-inducing way.

EXAMPLES OF HEALTHY COPING SKILLS

- Exercising and working out to release physical energy and increase "feel-good" chemicals.

- Sharing about your stress or problem with a trusted person.

- Getting professional counseling.

- Relying on your community or social network and connecting with others for support.

- Eating healthy and practicing good nutrition habits.

- Learning relaxation methods or practicing mindfulness.[2]

- Setting healthy boundaries, learning to say no, and communicating what you need to others.

- Engaging in spiritual practices such as prayer, worship, and meditating on Scripture.

In 2 Corinthians 4:8-9, the apostle Paul wrote, "We are hard pressed on every side, but not crushed; perplexed, but not in despair; persecuted, but not abandoned; struck down, but not destroyed." Especially during times in my life that have felt the most pressing, this passage has reminded me that no matter what era of history we're living in, there are circumstances and hardships that press up against us—to the point where we feel we might implode.

But the promise here is for us: *We will not be crushed.* No matter what pressure you are facing in your life right now, God has given you everything you need to come out healthier, stronger, more equipped, and more capable on the other side. The pressure cannot crush you, because of the Spirit of God at work inside you. You were not made to be crushed; you were made to overcome. And overcome you will. But to do that, you need to assess the pressure—and release it in a healthy way.

> ### VERSE FOR REFLECTION
>
> "We are hard pressed on every side, but not crushed; perplexed, but not in despair; persecuted, but not abandoned; struck down, but not destroyed" (2 Corinthians 4:8-9).

TODAY'S HABIT: IDENTIFY YOUR COPING SKILLS

1. Looking at the list above for ideas, write down a few unhealthy coping mechanisms that you tend to default to. Give specific examples of how and when you engage in these unhealthy coping skills.

2. Taking a look at the list above for ideas, write down two healthy coping mechanisms you'd like to practice instead. Write down specific examples of your plan of action: "When I feel stressed this coming week I will _____
   _____."

FEEL FREE TO FEEL

IDENTIFY YOUR EMOTIONS

I had an on-air counseling session on my podcast with a pastor who had spent most of his life avoiding difficult emotions. He didn't realize that by doing so, he was avoiding the joy of feeling altogether.

He grew up with a younger brother who displayed a lot of emotions, and he watched his brother get picked on, bullied, and harassed. He interpreted that by believing that to be vulnerable with your emotions is to be weak, and he made a pact with himself that he would always stay strong by keeping his feelings capped. Until one day, the cap broke. And the feelings he had been harboring for years all came to the surface for the very first time.

During our session, we traced back where his false beliefs about emotions came from and how he'd suppressed his emotions as a coping mechanism. But then we talked about the downside to capping your emotions: the inhibition of intimacy, joy, peace, hope, and connection. He didn't even realize how many wonderful emotions he had been missing until he finally started feeling the hard ones.[1]

I don't think I realized how many people were uncomfortable with emotions until I became a therapist. But the fascinating thing is that emotional discomfort looks very different in different people. So different that you might not even recognize it as discomfort. You can genuinely think you're comfortable with your emotions when you really aren't. Here are some signs that you might be uncomfortable with emotions:

- Have you ever started crying, and immediately tried to cover up your face or found yourself saying, "I'm sorry," apologizing for your display of feelings?

- Have you ever sat with someone as they shared something sad or difficult or confrontational, and found yourself holding back a smile or a laugh?

- When someone gives you a compliment, have you ever found yourself feeling uncomfortable and not sure how to respond or react?

- Do you tend to try to avoid conflict or confrontation in your relationships?

- Does anger seem to be the easiest emotion for you to express?

- Do you have a tendency to try to distract or numb yourself when you're "not feeling good"?

- Have you ever had the thought that you or someone else being emotional was a sign of weakness or a lack of control?

Maybe you're not as comfortable with emotions as you think you are. And that's okay, because there's a learning curve for all of us.

REWIRING OUR DEFAULT MODE

It would make sense that our default mode is to get away from uncomfortable or difficult things. It's how we survive in other areas of life. When you touch a hot stove, you automatically pull back your hand. When something suddenly scares you, you jump away in self-protection. In a way, your default mode is to protect yourself from harmful things. Not only are we wired to avoid uncomfortable experiences as an act of self-preservation, but we're also taught to avoid uncomfortable or difficult emotions due to avoidant patterns that have been passed down to us by our families, communities, and culture.

The problem is that we often confuse *uncomfortable* for *harmful*. But just because something is uncomfortable or difficult doesn't mean it's harmful. In fact, many difficult and uncomfortable things are good for us—if we'll lean into them instead of avoiding them.

Take, for example, a hard workout at the gym. I've been strength training regularly for about six months now, and let me tell you, that last set of reps often feels extremely uncomfortable and very difficult. My default mode would be to avoid feeling that level of discomfort at all costs; and for a season, I did. But now I'm allowing myself to feel the discomfort, knowing that it means I'm strengthening my muscles. I'm getting stronger. I'm pushing myself through the difficulty because it's producing a better me.

Your emotional muscles also need a good workout. Just because something feels difficult or uncomfortable doesn't mean it should be avoided. Feelings in and of themselves are not "bad or good"—it's what we do with those feelings. Learning to feel what we feel, pushing through the discomfort, is producing an emotional strength and courage that we need to be emotionally healthy people. You've got to give yourself permission. You've got to feel free to feel.

How often do you lean into what you or what others around you are feeling, and how quick are you to pull away?

FEEL FREE TO FEEL

Jesus was emotional.

Have you ever thought about that before? Out of all the words we use to describe Jesus—powerful, almighty, sovereign, compassionate— do we ever think to call Him emotional? That word probably doesn't make it on the typical list of qualities we use to describe Jesus. But He was a man who felt deeply and experienced meaningful and significant emotions here on this earth. In fact, Bible scholars have identified more than 39 different emotions Jesus expressed in His time on earth, from anger to agony to grief and sorrow to compassion and love and joy.[2] And that's just what we know from Scripture, not to mention the rest of His day-in-day-out life. John 21:25 tells us that if everything that Jesus did was written down, all the books in the world wouldn't be able to contain the stories. There's so much more to Jesus, so much more than we even know. But even in the glimpse we get of Him, we see that Jesus allowed Himself to feel, and He understood the importance of acknowledging and expressing what He felt. He modeled to us what it looks like to feel, and in doing so, He gave us permission to be in tune with our own feelings.

Jesus felt joy. (John 15:10-11)

Jesus felt sorrow. (Luke 19:41)

Jesus felt grief. (John 11:35)

Jesus felt exhaustion. (John 4:6)

Jesus felt anger. (Matthew 23:33)

Jesus felt compassion. (Matthew 9:36)

Jesus felt agony. (Luke 22:44)

And just like Jesus, we can be intentional about feeling deeply and responding gracefully. It's a muscle we have to build by allowing ourselves to lean into the discomfort rather than distracting, ignoring, numbing, or pushing it away.

What about you? Do you allow yourself to feel? Do you recognize your feelings? Not just the "easy" feelings like joy and excitement, but the hard ones like grief and loneliness too? How often do you lean into what you or what others around you are feeling, and how quick are you to pull away? If feeling the difficult feelings is part of the necessary strengthening of our emotional muscles, we'll also experience the reward of stronger, richer, more powerful positive emotions on the other side.

At the other end of the very same emotions that bring discomfort and pain are feelings that bring fulfillment, satisfaction, and healing. When you feel deeply on one side, you'll also feel deeply on the other side. Because on the other side of deep anxiety, there is deep peace. On the other side of strong sorrow, there is strong joy. On the other side of overwhelming heartache, there is overwhelming gratitude. "Weeping may last through the night, but joy comes with the morning" (Psalm 30:5 NLT). The hard feelings are often the catalyst for the easier feelings. And you can't have one set without the other. So feel free to feel.

VERSE FOR REFLECTION

"He was deeply moved in spirit and troubled...Jesus wept" (John 11:33, 35).

TODAY'S HABIT: IDENTIFY YOUR EMOTIONS

1. Visit www.DebraFileta.com/resources for a list of emotions
   to refer to for today's habit. Take some time to read through
   the list, then identify and list three uncomfortable or difficult feelings you've had in the past week:

   »

   »

   »

2. Was your tendency to lean into and learn from the feeling?
   Or did you avoid and withdraw from the feeling?

3. What action or behavior did you choose in response to that
   feeling?

4. For the next few weeks, make it a habit to mentally stop one
   time during the week to review today's daily practice, identify feelings that come up, and notice your response to those
   feelings. You may need to refer to the list of emotions frequently until you've got the vocabulary you need to mentally identify your emotions.

19

NECESSARY INTERRUPTIONS

UNDERSTAND THAT EMOTIONS ARE SIGNALS

can't stand interruptions.

Especially when I'm in the middle of something important or time sensitive, which is why I noticed a story about a family getting interrupted by a door-to-door salesman while they were hurriedly trying to leave their house for vacation. Not only was it bad timing, but the salesman also just so happened to be trying to sell them a same-day installation for a carbon monoxide alarm, trying to convince the wife that even though she was about to pack up her family and leave for vacation, this was the day to get it installed. The promise was that if they agreed, the installation team would be there and working on it within five minutes.

Even though the couple lived in a state where carbon monoxide alarms were not required, something about the exchange made them agree to do it. Maybe it was just to get the salesman to go away so they could get back to preparing for vacation (or maybe that tells you more about what happens in my head than anything else!). Either way, the installation team arrived and got to work, and the family was soon off to their trip.

After their time away, the family arrived back home late at night and quickly got to bed. In the middle of the night, the couple was awakened by an alarm going off, accompanied by a call from the alarm system operator saying carbon monoxide had been detected in the home. It seemed like something was faulty, since the alarm system had just been installed a few days before. But when the alarm wouldn't stop, the husband was advised to call the fire department. Within moments of being in the home, the firefighters called for an emergency evacuation, as the carbon monoxide levels were off the charts before the firefighters had even reached the basement.

When the family was outside, one of the firefighters pulled them aside. I watched a video of the homeowner telling the story, and with tears in his eyes he recalled the words the firefighter had told him: "The levels were high enough that if you hadn't paid attention to the alarm, you would be dead in the morning."[1]

Talk about a necessary interruption. If it hadn't been for that alarm system, the entire family wouldn't have seen another day.

You have a built-in alarm system as well. It's called your sympathetic nervous system. This is your fight-or-flight response that sends messages to your brain and chemicals throughout your body that tell you something needs attention. Your emotions are an important part of this system. They are the alarm—the signal your body uses to prompt a response. This built-in system can save your life. Your fight-or-flight response kicks into action in times of heightened emotion or distress—when you're crossing a dangerously busy street, when you hear a noise in the middle of the night, or when you're in the middle of a heated argument. All these situations send signals to your body, giving you a chance to act and respond. A chance to keep yourself safe and secure.

Even when you don't have a heightened fight-or-flight response, every emotion in your body is a sign cluing you in to what is going on underneath the surface, and we need to be in tune to the signals.

A signal's job is to tell you, *There's something more going on here.*

HOW DOES THAT MAKE YOU FEEL?

Why is it that the stereotypical question you hear from a therapist in any movie or TV show is, "How does that make you feel?" We therapists seem to be all about the *feelings*. And I'll admit, part of that is true. Because your feelings are essentially a part of a bigger equation, pointing you to other experiences that might be going on inside you and around you.

This is why recognizing our feelings as signals is crucial to understanding the bigger picture of why we do what we do. If that portion of the equation is missing, we're not going to have much insight into or control over how we behave. Here are some examples of how someone can feel an emotion and react to the emotion itself, rather than understanding the emotion as a signal and responding accordingly.

- Mike was feeling overwhelmed, so he snapped at his wife and kids even though they hadn't done anything wrong.

- Kelsey was feeling insecure, so she lied about her job to make herself sound smarter.

- Ben was feeling stressed, so he blew some money shopping online even when it broke his budget.

- Susan was feeling desperate, so she gave him another chance even though he had broken her heart before.

- Trey was feeling guilty, so he said yes to the meeting even though it took away more time from his family.

REACTING TO FEELINGS VERSUS RESPONDING TO EMOTIONS

So much of what we do is driven by a reaction to how we *feel*. You feel something, so you act a certain way. The problem is, we don't often take the time to process or identify *why* we're feeling that way. What is this feeling telling me? What is it signaling to me? We tend to want to quickly brush away the "bad feelings," so we do whatever we can to make them go away as fast as possible. We *react* to our feelings instead of *responding* to our feelings. *Reacting* means we act quickly or thoughtlessly just to make the feeling go away. *Responding* means we take the time to figure out what we're feeling and what it might be telling us, and then act in a healthy way that helps to alleviate that feeling. *Responding* means we pay attention to feelings—both positive and negative—as we navigate through life. Scripture reminds us that there is a time for both—because both are signals.

A signal's job is to tell you, *There's something more going on here.* When we can pause and actually process what's going on—what we're feeling and why and what we might need to do about it—we realize we have options. We realize there's a reason we're feeling what we feel, and we can make a positive choice in response. Let's look back at some of the examples above and see what it looks like to understand that feelings are signals, and we can respond to those signals in a healthy way:

- Mike was feeling overwhelmed, so he realized there was too much on his plate and began coming up with ways to alleviate some of that pressure.

- Kelsey was feeling insecure, so she realized that she was believing the lie that she wasn't good enough and worked hard to change her mindset and beliefs about herself.

- Ben was feeling stressed, so he realized he'd been putting unrealistic expectations on himself and decided to set better boundaries with the people in his life.

- Susan was feeling desperate, so she realized she had been living in isolation for far too long and committed to being intentional about investing in healthy friendships.

- Trey was feeling guilty, so he realized he was taking responsibility for how others might feel rather than prioritizing his family and decided to make some changes.

Remember: you have the power to either react or respond. Don't tune out your feelings as if they're some unnecessary interruption. Because they just might be telling you something. Something that could even save your life.

VERSE FOR REFLECTION

"There is a time for everything…a time to weep, and a time to laugh" (Ecclesiastes 3:1, 4).

TODAY'S HABIT: UNDERSTAND THAT EMOTIONS ARE SIGNALS

---

1. What are some ways you react instead of respond to your feelings?

List the three feelings you noticed from the last daily practice.

»

»

»

2. If feelings are signals, what might those feelings be trying to signal to you?

   Example:

   > **Feeling:** Overwhelmed

   > **Signal:** I'm doing too much and need to set better boundaries.

   > **Feeling:**

   > **Signal:**

   > **Feeling:**

   > **Signal:**

   > **Feeling:**

   > **Signal:**

20

FALSE ALARMS

QUESTION YOUR EMOTIONS

A near-death experience has side effects. As I've shared in another book, an unexpected and traumatic miscarriage led me to lose so much blood that I was minutes away from death. Emergency surgery saved my life.

That experience stayed with me, hibernating under the surface of my life for a few years until one day, it burst through in the form of my first of many panic attacks. Trauma tends to stay in our bodies in the form of physical or emotional angst until we finally allow ourselves to pay attention to it—to deal with it.

In our last lesson, we talked about the importance of understanding emotions as signals. I shared with you about our sympathetic nervous system, and how its job is to alert us to something that needs our attention through a fight-or-flight response in our bodies. The part of the brain that's involved in that process is called our *amygdala*. It's the emotional response center in our brain, and it also stores and retrieves emotional memories. It groups them into categories to help us differentiate dangerous experiences from ordinary ones. But every now and again, it gets something wrong. It can take an emotion we're feeling in the present and make us think we're in danger because of something we've experienced in the past. It's like a *false* alarm.

This especially happens for those of us who have some sort of trauma in our past. We can feel something in the present that our amygdala identifies as a threat. Just because you hear an alarm doesn't mean there's always a fire. With our amygdala, it might just mean there was a fire a long time ago. The key is looking for other clues and information to differentiate the real alarms from the false alarms.

My amygdala started false-alarming a few years after my traumatic miscarriage. Anytime I would feel something uncomfortable in my body—a headache, a little dizziness from dehydration, my heart racing after a workout—I would start to feel extremely afraid that I was going to die. My amygdala would automatically assume I was back in a place of danger, and my body would go into fight-or-flight mode. Even when I was safe. Even when I was healthy. Even when everything was okay. I couldn't conceptualize all this at first, or put it into words, but all I knew is that my anxiety would spike, and I'd find myself in the middle of a panic attack.

Just because you hear an alarm
doesn't mean there's always a fire.

REAL BUT NOT TRUE

I realized my sympathetic nervous system was being affected by my past trauma. So I got plugged into therapy for myself and started reading and learning as much as I could about what was happening in my body and brain during a panic attack. Through all my learning, the concept that stuck with me most is this: Just because you feel something doesn't make it true. Your feelings are real, but they aren't always true.

Sometimes your feelings are informed by your past, your trauma, and your previous experiences rather than the truth of what's happening here and now. When I say your feelings are real, I mean that they are telling you something. Your feelings are real because they're signals. For me, the signal of anxiety I was feeling years after my miscarriage didn't mean I was actually dying, but it did mean I had trauma in my past from which I still needed to heal. I had to learn to differentiate the real alarms, informed by truth, from the false alarms, informed by trauma. The truth was that I was okay, I was safe, and I was healthy. The truth was that I had been through something really difficult, and I needed to be intentional about engaging in the process of healing from that past trauma.

FEELINGS CAN'T ALWAYS BE TRUSTED

This is all so important for us today because we live in a culture that tells us straight up to follow our feelings. Rather than see them as *signals*, we're told to see them as *truth*. Our truth. The truth. We're encouraged to own our truth no matter how it affects the people around us. But that's not the message I see in Scripture. God's Word highlights the value and importance of our emotions as signals, but it never elevates them to the level of truth. *Just because you feel something doesn't make it true.*

My eyes were opened to the importance of all of this while I was healing from my past trauma and facing my journey with panic attacks. I came across the passage in Scripture where Jesus was praying in the garden of Gethsemane, moments before He was captured to be taken to the cross. The Bible says He was in such agony that He began to sweat droplets of blood. Medical experts have identified this condition as *hematidrosis*, an extremely rare physical reaction that's likely related to a fight-or-flight response. His body was under such emotional distress that it signaled His sympathetic system to respond. The alarms were going off, telling Him to get out of there, to run in the other direction. But Jesus knew this: Though His feelings couldn't always be trusted, His God could always be trusted. Even though everything inside Him was telling Him to run, Jesus decided to stay and offer His life as a sacrifice for me and for you.

I want to turn this all around and help you understand that the same goes for you and the things you feel. Your feelings are real signals, but they aren't always telling you the truth. Sometimes those signals are false alarms, informed by past trauma. To become emotionally healthy, it's important that we engage in the process of questioning our emotions rather than simply reacting to them.

Just because you feel lonely doesn't mean you're really alone.

Just because you feel worthless doesn't mean you're lacking in value.

Just because you feel afraid doesn't mean there's something to fear.

Just because you feel inadequate doesn't mean you don't have what it takes.

Just because you feel useless doesn't mean you lack significance.

Just because you feel hopeless doesn't mean there's no hope.

Just because you feel overwhelmed doesn't mean you're not capable.

Just because you feel something doesn't make it true.

Be on the lookout for false alarms, because they're a signal—a signal that there's more healing to be received.

VERSE FOR REFLECTION

"Being in anguish, he prayed more earnestly, and his sweat was like drops of blood falling to the ground" (Luke 22:44).

TODAY'S HABIT: QUESTION YOUR EMOTIONS

1. Take some time to journal about feelings that come up in your life that may not be the truth about your life or situation. Look at the list above as a reference for ideas and use the format "Just because I feel _____ doesn't mean _____" as you write about your own false alarms.

2. Could these false alarms be a sign that there's more healing to receive? How so?

21

TRIGGERS ARE EVERYWHERE

RECOGNIZE WHAT SETS YOU OFF

We live in a trigger-avoidant culture. We don't want to get near anything that might set us off, anything that will make us feel anything less than content. The message we get from culture is to just cut off the trigger-inducing person or experience rather than heal the trigger itself. Does that person trigger you? Cut them out of your life. Does that sermon trigger you? Stop going to that church. Does that book trigger you? Throw it in the garbage. We want to run away from whatever makes us feel uncomfortable, but then we tend to run toward distractions, addictions, and compulsions that numb us instead.

But what if triggers were the very thing that invited us into the process of healing? What if they actually revealed our sore spots—the emotional wounds in our lives that need tending to?

What are triggers? To put it simply: A trigger is any word, action, thought, interaction, or experience that elicits or provokes an overwhelming negative emotional response. They're things that "set us off." Something someone says can be a trigger. It could be something you see, or hear, or taste, or touch, or think, or read, or feel.

A phrase I often use to explain the concept of triggers is "emotional sore spots." Sore spots are usually the result of an injury. If you've ever noticed a black-and-blue bruise on your body, it's a sign of a previous hurt. Sometimes you can clearly remember the source of that hurt—like the time I slammed my shoulder into the hard edge of the coatrack in a rush on my way out the door. But other times, you might find a bruise, but you aren't acutely aware of where it came from. But whether you can identify the source or not, both types of sore spots have one thing in common: they cause pain. Even though they're wounds from the past, bruises are still sensitive to the touch because they hurt when they're pressed.

Emotional sore spots are similar; they're signs that point to previous pain or hurts or wounds from your past. Emotional sore spots are sensitive to the touch; they hurt when they're pressed. Triggers in the present tend to press on sore spots from the past. It could be...

> the scent of a certain cologne, bringing sorrow as it reminds you your husband is no longer there.

> a song playing on the radio, overwhelming you with heartbreak as it reminds you of a relationship that once was but no longer is.

> the confrontation you had with your boss, filling you with the same insecurities you felt in the presence of your controlling father.

> an argument you had with your spouse, reminding you of the sting of rejection you felt as a child.

Triggers are everywhere. And as much as they clue us in to what's happening in the present, they're also evidence of something deeper. A sore spot that needs attention. Triggers are a sign that there's more healing to be received. They're a sign that God is not done, and He's still working. They're a sign that there are new levels of healing available. The important thing is that we recognize our triggers and not allow our lives to be dictated by them. That we acknowledge them and bring them to the surface for healing, rather than working to simply avoid them.

Triggers are a sign that there's more healing to be received.

All throughout Scripture we're reminded that God wants to coat our lives with His overwhelming and supernatural peace. But you and I both know there are obstacles that get in the way of that peace. Triggers themselves don't keep us from that peace—in fact, they help us identify what is getting in the way so we can give it our attention and lean into the process of healing.

What does it look like to search your heart and life for triggers, and realize that you are strong, alive, and capable of doing the work of healing? What does it look like to lean into the triggers, recognizing them as an invitation for healing?

God is not finished with His work in your life. There's more to be received. If that's the case, I say, "Bring it on, Lord. Bring it on. Heal all the broken and hurting places like only You can do. Spotlight the things that need to be healed and flood our lives with Your peace."

VERSE FOR REFLECTION

"Let the peace of Christ rule in your hearts" (Colossians 3:15).

TODAY'S HABIT: RECOGNIZE WHAT SETS YOU OFF

1. Identify one or more triggers in your life: any word, action, thought, interaction, or experience that elicits or provokes an overwhelming negative emotional response.

2. What might be the emotional sore spot underneath the surface?

3. What area in your life could that trigger be revealing that needs more healing?

22

FEELINGS IN MY BODY

TUNE IN TO THE PHYSICAL IMPACT OF EMOTIONS

You store feelings in your body.

Essentially, your body is like a container, holding all those emotions inside. Those feelings release neurochemicals that are deposited in the makeup of your body and affect it in both the short term as well as in the long term. So what you feel emotionally ends up affecting what you're feeling physically, both now and later in life. Your positive emotions release feel-good chemicals, and your negative emotions release stress chemicals.

Sometimes you can see and feel the effects of certain emotions in your body immediately. Have you ever been worried or anxious about something and found yourself having stomach pain, nausea, or digestive issues? Maybe you've gotten extremely angry and felt like your body was heating up, your heart rate spiking, and your face flushed red. Even more obvious are the effects of feelings of sadness or sorrow, which can cause physical tears. Water literally starts flowing from your eyes! If that alone doesn't prove to us how deeply connected our emotions are with our physical bodies, then I don't know what does. Scientists are still trying to understand the uniquely human trait that is crying, but it's been identified as a self-soothing physical response causing stress reduction, mood enhancement, and physical relief.[1] These are just some of the ways emotions impact our body in the short term.

Not only that, but emotions stored in the body can have long-lasting effects. People who have more positive feelings contained in their bodies have actually been proven to live longer.[2] On the flip side, those who harbor feelings like stress and anxiety have a much higher likelihood of experiencing long-term negative effects, from memory loss to cognitive impairment (deficits in decision-making, attention, judgment, and learning). Not only that, but harboring stress can cause impairment of your immune system, causing you to get sick more often than people who aren't stressed; impairment of your cardiovascular system, affecting the function of your heart; impairment of your gastrointestinal system, effecting your digestive process; and impairment of your endocrine system, changing the balance of hormones being released in your body.[3] When you put it like this, you realize how important your feelings actually are, and how powerful it is to be aware of the feelings you're storing in your body.

Emotions stored in the body can have long-lasting effects.

THE BODY SCAN

When I work with children in the therapeutic setting, I'll have them do an activity called "Feelings in My Body." I ask them to draw an outline of their body and then color in the places where they feel different emotions in their body. A similar study was done with a group of 700 adults who were given a silhouette of a human body and asked to map out the places they felt stimulated in their body as they were being exposed to a series of response-provoking prompts.[4] Scientists used this data to literally map out similarities of places where human beings feel the effect of certain emotions in their bodies. It's the body's way of telling us there's an emotion that needs to be acknowledged and dealt with.

The habit of scanning your body for emotions is an important process, and one we use often in the counseling office in an activity called progressive muscle relaxation. It helps us slow down, take the time to recognize how our emotions might be affecting our bodies, and try to relieve some of that tension. You've probably heard the question, "Where do you carry your stress?" Certain parts of the body tend to tense up or react as a response to underlying emotions. So being in tune with our body is another important way we can be in tune with our feelings. In today's habit, you'll take a few minutes to do a body scan and get in touch with the feelings in your body.

VERSE FOR REFLECTION

"You created my inmost being; you knit me together in my mother's womb. I praise you because I am fearfully and wonderfully made; your works are wonderful, I know that full well" (Psalm 139:13-14).

TODAY'S HABIT: TUNE IN TO THE PHYSICAL IMPACT OF EMOTIONS

---

1. Set aside ten minutes for today's activity. Find a comfortable chair in a quiet location where you won't be interrupted. Close your eyes and take one minute to deeply breathe in and out.

2. With your eyes still closed, take one minute to scan your head, starting from the top of your head and going down to your chin. Tune into any sensations you might be feeling in this area of your body (such as a headache in the forehead area, sinus pain in the nasal area, fluid in your ears, or tingling on your lips).

3. Next, take one minute to tune into your body from your neck down to your shoulders, being aware of any physical

sensations such as temperature (hot or cold) or tension (tight muscles).

4. Lastly, take four minutes to scan the rest of your body from your shoulders down to your toes, taking a few moments to isolate each section of the body as you scan for any sensations, tension, pain, or general discomfort.

5. Full body: After you finish your body scan, close your eyes again and from the top of your head down to the bottom of your toes, try to pinpoint areas that might become activated with certain emotions. For example: *When I feel anxious, I sense pressure in my chest. When I feel mad, I sense heat down my head and neck.* Return to this full-body practice after you feel a strong emotion throughout the next few weeks and see if you can make any observations as you scan your body for emotions.

WORK IT OUT

FIND BODY-MIND OUTLETS

What you think influences how you feel, which in turn influences how you live. In other words, your mental and emotional health affects your biological functioning. Understanding the fact that stored emotions are affecting your body is an important first step, but figuring out what to do with those emotions is a necessary second step. When we talk about the body-mind connection, we're talking about how the body affects your mental and emotional world and vice versa. Now that we understand the cycle and know what we're looking for, let's talk about what to do with it. You're going to need methods to "un-store" emotions (such as stress, anxiety, anger, and depression) by finding healthy outlets to release those feelings back into the world. We need to find outlets for the body and outlets for the mind.

What you're really doing is *working it out*—
working out the stress, the pain, the overwhelm,
the lies, the insecurities, the fears.

BODY OUTLET: PHYSICAL ACTIVITY

Too many people underestimate the power of physical activity on their mental and emotional health. According to a report from the CDC, only 23 percent of Americans are getting the recommended amount of physical activity they need—150 minutes of moderate exercise per week, or 75 minutes of vigorous exercise per week in addition to muscle-strengthening activities two or more days per week.[1] That comes out to about 30 minutes, 5 times a week of moderate exercise or 25 minutes 3 times a week of vigorous exercise.

Not only is exercise an important component to physical health and resilience (reducing causes of mortality by up to 30 percent), but it's a crucial component to mental and emotional health and resilience.[2] Studies show that physical exercise can reduce your body's reaction to stress-inducing situations by affecting your body's fight-or-flight response.[3] Not only that, but regular physical activity essentially increases the feel-good chemicals in your body, all while decreasing the release of the stress chemicals.[4] This is why exercise is seen as such an important part of the equation of your mental and emotional health. In some studies, regular exercise was shown to be just as effective in the treatment of depression as the use of an antidepressant.[5] Holistic healing means we look at every piece of the puzzle, from changing our diet and exercise habits, to engaging in therapy and lifestyle changes, to assessing our need for medication. They all work together, moving us in the direction of healing.

Many people have found that regular exercise is a huge component to their commitment of pursuing both physical and mental-emotional health. Christine Caine says that even when she travels, "I run, hike, or jump on an elliptical machine in a hotel fitness room, depending on where I am. Nothing helps me get over jet lag and be able to focus better than exercise. I don't ask myself if I feel like doing it, I just do it." It's like taking your daily dose of medication: You don't just do it when you feel like it or when you're particularly motivated. You do it because it's an essential part of keeping yourself healthy.

MIND OUTLET: TALK THERAPY

I've used the analogy of seeing the working out of your emotional health just like you see the process of working out for physical fitness. In both situations, you've got to do the work. But what you're really doing is *working it out*—working out the stress, the pain, the overwhelm, the lies, the insecurities, the fears. You're working it out of your system, making room for new, healthier, better methods of feeling, thinking, and behaving.

And this is why I truly believe in the power of professional counseling, also known as *talk therapy*. It's the emotional outlet for all those things you have going on inside. It helps you sort through your thoughts, stay in tune to your emotions, and replace your behaviors. Time and time again, psychotherapy has been proven to impact overall functioning and quality of life.[6] It changes things, because it changes you! It begins to strengthen your mental and emotional muscles, increasing your capacity to handle intrapersonal problems and interpersonal relationships. It gets you stronger from the inside out.

As you look at creating powerful habits that help you work out both your physical and mental world, take inventory of the outlets you're creating for yourself today. How much time are you committing to working it out both physically and mentally? What steps can you take to begin prioritizing your health from the inside out?

VERSE FOR REFLECTION

"Do you not know that your bodies are temples of the Holy Spirit, who is in you, whom you have received from God?" (1 Corinthians 6:19).

TODAY'S HABIT: FIND BODY-MIND OUTLETS

1. How many minutes do you spend per week in physical activity? _____

2. What is one step you can take toward increasing your physical activity levels this week? (*Suggestions*: Track your steps each day and try to hit 10,000 steps, walk during a part of your lunch break, find an equipment-free workout plan online to work out from your living room, actively play outside with your kids instead of indoors, go on "walk-dates" with friends instead of coffee dates, and take a morning prayer run before you get ready for the day.)

3. What have you built into your life as a mental-emotional outlet? Consider working with a counselor by visiting www.DebraFileta.com/counseling for counseling resources and the opportunity to connect with me and my team at the Debra Fileta Counselors Network.

LIVING FULL TO FULLY LIVE

PRACTICE SOUL-CARE

What fills you up?
You might be able to answer right away, but maybe you need to take a few moments to think about it. If that's the case, please do. My next question for you is this: How full do you feel right now? In this moment? The answer to these questions changes everything and points us in the direction of what it really looks like to care for yourself.

I recently worked with a thirtysomething woman we'll call Madeline. She was going through a hard time, feeling empty, stuck, and discontent in her life. There was nothing "bad" about her life, but she also wasn't enjoying life. As we dug a little deeper, it was pretty evident that most of her life revolved around meeting the needs of others. She faithfully served in multiple ministries at church. Her parents were divorced, and so she responsibly stepped in to care for her ailing father's physical needs as well as her lonely mother's emotional needs. She was the oldest of four siblings and was always there when they needed a place to stay, a shoulder to cry on, money to borrow, or just a place to vent. She was there for everybody else—except herself. And finally, it all came to a head. Madeline was feeling drained, depressed, and depleted. She felt like she had nothing more to give. And when you put your entire life's value and worth in the sum of what you can give, it makes sense why she was feeling so miserable.

The real work of healing began for Madeline as we started to get to the root of *why*.

"Why do you take that role in everyone's life? When did this begin? What underlying thoughts and beliefs do you have that make you feel guilty, responsible, and obligated to be the 'one' for everyone else? What underlying thoughts and beliefs do you have that make you feel selfish, rude, and ashamed when you begin thinking about your own needs?" The practices and habits throughout this book were exactly what we used to do some of this work with Madeline. Working through her timeline, Madeline was able to identify that some of these patterns started way back in childhood, in a dysfunctional and chaotic home environment where she constantly felt that she had to fill in the gaps for her parents, who couldn't seem to ever get along. She thought, *If I don't do it, no one else will. If I don't fix it, something bad will happen.* She started getting to the roots of some of those beliefs she'd carried for far too long, beliefs that were preventing her from setting healthy boundaries and learning to care for herself. She realized, "I guess I'm still trying to fix everything for everyone to this day." Her eyes began to open to the *why* as she unpacked her history.

"Even after giving my life to Jesus, I've continued to believe that I am somehow responsible for everyone else. I'm afraid that if I don't fix things, they'll fall apart, and in the end I'll be alone. Ironically, I'm feeling very alone right now."

This, right here, my friend, is the beginning of real change. It's not just about what we do, but *why* we do it. I could have easily told Madeline to give a little less time to ministry, say no to her siblings a little more often, and go get a manicure once a week—and all of that may have a role at a later time. But if we're not really getting to the roots of the why, replacing false beliefs with truth and understanding the signals our feelings are sending us, we'll just default back to old behaviors. In this case, the behavior that needed to change was Madeline's ability to tend to her own soul—her commitment to care for herself. And she started taking real and lasting steps toward change, from the inside out.

Self-care leads to soul-care.

Let's turn the tables for a moment. When you think of the word *self-care*, what's your gut reaction? If you had a negative response to that word, let's dig a little deeper. Maybe you have a hard time with the idea of self-care, assuming it's selfish to care about yourself in any capacity. But let me stop here: *Why* do you believe that? This is where pausing to get to the root of our underlying beliefs, and then looking for patterns in our thoughts and feelings, has the power to change our lives. It's not about simply recognizing that "I'm not into self-care," but asking why, and questioning those underlying thoughts and beliefs. What if we changed the word from *self-care* to *soul-care* instead? Would that bring about a different reaction for you? Because here's what you need to remember: When you're caring for yourself, you're caring for your soul.

How full do you feel today? How empty do you feel today? What does it look like to fulfill the responsibility of caring for yourself even as you care for others? Self-care is not an anti-Christian word. In fact, it's what's required for us to fill up and care for our souls. And to be healthy people, we need to be full people. When we stop caring for ourselves, we become empty, and you can't give to others out of what you don't have for yourself. This is why I believe Scripture is so deliberate in telling us to love your neighbor *as you love yourself* (Matthew 22:39).

We can learn so much from what Jesus *didn't* say. Jesus could have easily commanded us to love our neighbor *more* than we love ourselves, but He didn't. He could have encouraged us to "love your neighbor *not* yourself." But He didn't. Because He knew that tending to our own hearts, souls, minds, and strength is an important part of filling up so we can continue to pour out. Not only that, but Jesus Himself modeled the power of soul-care!

- He set boundaries with people and took time to be alone with the Father. (Luke 5:16)

- He stopped to rest. (Mark 6:30-32)

- He took naps. (Mark 4:38)

- He took the time to nourish His body by eating and drinking. (Matthew 11:19)

- He made time to stop and celebrate. (Luke 22:7-8)

- He prioritized spending time with His friends. (John 13:23)

- He spent long hours in prayer. (Mark 1:35, 6:46)

Jesus was a person who functioned on F—the fullness of God—rather than on E—the emptiness of self. Take inventory today of how you're taking care of yourself, but more importantly, get to the root of the why. Because self-care leads to soul-care.

VERSE FOR REFLECTION

"Love your neighbor as yourself" (Matthew 22:39).

TODAY'S HABIT: PRACTICE SOUL-CARE

1. How full do you feel in this season of your life? (Zero being *I feel empty and drained*, ten being *I feel filled to overflowing*.)

2. What is your response to the word *self-care*? Why? What are your underlying thoughts or feelings about this concept?

3. If you struggle with self-care, what thoughts, beliefs, or feelings have prevented you from caring for yourself? Write out some ways you can begin to replace underlying beliefs with truth about self-care.

4. List two to three specific ways you want to care for yourself or "fill yourself up" in each of these four areas of your life. I've started you off with some examples.

   Emotionally: (time with life-giving relationships, counseling, time alone to recharge, finding a mentor)

   Spiritually: (meditating on Scripture, memorizing Scripture, time in God's Word, worship, prayer)

Mentally: (reading a book, taking a class for pleasure, watching a documentary, having stimulating conversations)

Physically: (picking up an active hobby, exercising regularly, taking a warm bath, taking time to sleep in, eating nutritiously, going for a walk)

HEALTHY WITHDRAWAL

UNPLUG

I have a love-hate relationship with batteries.

Don't get me wrong, I'm in complete awe that somehow in modern times we've been able to use technology to create small containers that actually hold energy for us to use as needed. But I'm also acutely aware that these little containers of energy can easily run out, and usually do at the most inconvenient times. In fact, in the middle of writing this book this very thing happened to me. When I write, I write. I put my head down and get deep into the process. My fingers fly at 120 words a minute, and my mind flies even faster. So fast, I don't stop to think about other things—including plugging in my laptop to a power source. I was so immersed in one section of the book that I didn't even see the yellow low-battery icon furiously blinking at me at the bottom of the screen. Until everything shut down. The entire screen turned black. My laptop battery was totally dead. And I found myself in panic mode because I couldn't for the life of me remember if I had hit Save before that last flurry of ideas had been put into words from page 23 to page 34. Like I said, I have a love-hate relationship with batteries. (I know you won't be able to focus on the rest of this chapter if I don't tell you what happened, so to ease your mind, when my laptop powered back up I realized I had preemptively put my document in "autosave" mode. So even though I didn't hit Save before it shut down—Jesus saves!)

LIMITED CAPACITY

In a way, you and I are like little containers of energy. We're human beings with limited capacity, strength, and resources. We can only put out so much before we go kaput. We run out because we've got a limited amount. And truth be told, we live in a culture where our human battery can be drained in more ways than any other time in history. We've got more demands than ever before, more roles to play, more hats to wear, more tasks to juggle, more opportunities to stretch us, more people who want our help, more ladders to climb, more things to fill our schedules, more needs in our world than can be met.

Add to that, we're walking around with one of the most draining pieces of technology in our back pockets at all times: our smartphones. Even with all the demands we're already dealing with, they still lure us into scrolling our feed just a little longer, Googling that next thing that popped into our head, binging on just one more episode on Netflix, watching just one more mindless YouTube video. It takes just a little more of what we're already lacking—our energy, our attention, our focus, our time. Interestingly, studies have shown that more time on social media is linked to increased feelings of social isolation.[1] The more we try to connect using social media, the less connected we feel. The more we try to "fill up" on things that don't actually satisfy, the more drained we are in the end.

Which is why we've got to be deliberate about learning to withdraw.

WITHDRAWAL VERSUS WITHDRAWAL

Withdrawal isn't always seen as a positive thing. Maybe it's because I'm immersed in the mental health world, but personally, when I hear the word *withdrawal*, I immediately think of the uncomfortable symptoms of weaning off a substance or medication. The next thing that comes to mind is the unhealthy coping mechanism of withdrawal: running or escaping from uncomfortable feelings rather than facing them and dealing with them. Maybe you've even seen glimpses of that form of withdrawal in your own life.

But there's a different kind of withdrawal—a healthy kind. This kind of withdrawal is a deliberate and intentional "unplugging" of the things that drain us in order to plug in and recharge in the presence of God. It's recognizing that we have limits and needs and taking the time to pull away so we can replenish. It's realizing that we have a limited capacity, and that our emotional battery will get drained if we're always pushing through and never looking for the yellow blinking light.

Out of all the healthy habits Jesus practiced in His life, the one that stands out the most is His habit to withdraw and pray (Mark 1:35, 6:46, 14:32-41; Luke 6:12, 9:18, 9:28, 11:1). He made it a regular part of His life to withdraw to lonely places to connect with God (Luke 5:16). Something tells me that if Jesus lived in the twenty-first century, He would be just as intentional, if not more, about unplugging from the demands and distractions of the world. Something tells me He would have made sure to turn His phone to *do not disturb*, silenced the ringer, and made it a habit to unplug from His devices for hours, even days at a time. An important part of being healthy people isn't just learning to fill up, but also learning to identify the things that drain us.

What would it look like for us to model this healthy habit of withdrawal by unplugging and being alone with God on a regular basis? Because no matter what we run to in this world, a deep filling can only come from the God who made us to be filled by Him. But we have to be deliberate about going there; we have to be deliberate about allowing ourselves to be filled. If Jesus Himself, who shared such intimacy with the Father, had to be intentional about withdrawing and unplugging in order to fill up, how much more do we?

A deep filling can only come from the God
who made us to be filled by Him.

SOLITUDE VERSUS ISOLATION

In my work as a professional counselor, one of the most significant fears I've observed from my clients is the fear of feeling alone. We're afraid of feeling invisible to the world. I wonder if this buried fear is what keeps some people stuck in a cycle of unhealthy relationships, desperately trying to fight the fear of loneliness. Maybe this fear is what keeps people so insatiably dependent on their phones, desperately trying to connect through the mechanism of social media. We want to be seen, to be felt, to be noticed. We want to matter.

But there's a difference between being alone and feeling alone. You can actually be alone, but not feel alone. That is the difference between solitude and loneliness. Solitude is the deliberate act of being by yourself: giving yourself a chance to think, to feel, and to fill up. Loneliness, on the other hand, is a state of mind—a feeling of disconnect from the people around you, that leaves you feeling drained and isolated in the end. Loneliness happens when we're unintentional. Solitude happens when we practice intentionality. We'll talk more about what it looks like to intentionally establish healthy connections a little later, but for now I want to zoom in on the discipline of solitude. Science and psychology are finally beginning to understand what Jesus understood long ago: There is power in solitude, including deeper creativity, intimacy, and spirituality.[2]

Solitude isn't simply about being by yourself, it's about what you do during that time. As one article explains:

> "It's a deeper internal process," notes Matthew Bowker, a psychoanalytic political theorist at Medaille College who has researched solitude. Productive solitude requires internal exploration, a kind of labor which can be uncomfortable, even excruciating. "It might take a little bit of work before it turns into a pleasant experience."[3]

For us as believers, it's not just time alone—it's time in God's presence. Jesus didn't just withdraw to lonely places; He "withdrew to lonely places and prayed" (Luke 5:16). He pulled away to come close.

He unplugged to reconnect. He withdrew to draw closer to the only One who could fill Him up.

What does it look like for you to withdraw from the distractions, demands, and difficulties of this world? What does it look like for you to carve out time to pursue solitude? The life of Jesus so clearly challenges us to unplug so we can stay connected. So let me ask you this: What's keeping you from unplugging?

VERSE FOR REFLECTION

"Jesus often withdrew to lonely places and prayed" (Luke 5:16).

TODAY'S HABIT: UNPLUG

1. What are the demands, difficulties, and distractions keeping you from intentionally withdrawing in solitude?

2. Do you resonate with the "fear of feeling alone"? If so, try to identify a few ways being alone triggers deeper feelings or beliefs about yourself. *Example: Being alone makes me feel like I'm not wanted.*

3. "There's a difference between being alone and feeling alone."
   When do you feel most alone? How can you turn that time
   of feeling alone into an opportunity for solitude and connection with God?

4. Take 30 to 60 minutes today (or this week) to clear a portion of your schedule and be intentional about unplugging
   from your usual devices. Go to a quiet, relaxing place. Consider making this place your go-to space for solitude in the
   future. (You may have to try a few places before you find
   "your place.") Bring a journal to write in and then spend
   some time alone with God, praying and reading Scripture.
   If you don't know what to write in your journal, feel free to
   use these prompts to help get you started:

   > **God, thank You for…** (Spend some time in gratitude for
   > who God is and what He's given you.)
   >
   > **I am really struggling with…** (Be honest with God about
   > sins, struggles, or needs in your life and make time to
   > confess what you've done wrong and where you need His
   > forgiveness or His strength.)
   >
   > **I'm worried/afraid/frustrated/angry about…** (Share your
   > feelings with Him and don't hold back.)
   >
   > **A verse that stuck out to me from my Scripture reading
   > today is…** (Open the Word and see what He might be
   > speaking to your heart through it.)
   >
   > **It meant something to me because…** (Why was this
   > passage meaningful to you?)

This is what I believe You are teaching and showing me through Your Word...(What do you think God wants to tell you through your reading today?)

I want to pray for...(Spend some time in prayer for specific people or for specific needs you might have.)

Thank You for making me...(List the ways God has uniquely made you—your strengths, giftings, calling.)

Help me to...(What do you have coming up ahead that you need God's help with? Or what's something you're working on changing? Where do you need breakthrough, motivation, consistency, or a reset in your life?)

THE 8:8:8 RULE

REST

T ime management is an oxymoron.

You can't manage time because time is outside of your control. It keeps on ticking regardless of whether you want it to. You can't control time, so, when we say "time management" what we really mean is this: priorities. What you prioritize will take up your time. And we humans have the uncanny ability to get our priorities out of order. Which is why we scroll instead of sleeping. Work instead of playing. Grind instead of connecting. A look at some of the idioms our culture commonly uses is eerily telling: *hustle, grind, go all out, do all the things, dog-eat-dog, go the extra mile, climb the ladder, chase the paper, go hard.* We live in a world where to do more means to have more means to be more, which ironically, is the recipe for burnout and depression.

And this isn't new for us. We've been confusing our priorities since the beginning of our history. Which is exactly why the 8:8:8 rule was introduced. This concept dates to the industrial revolution, when factories were requiring their workers to work up to 16-hour days, six days a week, in an attempt to increase production. In 1817, a Welsh manufacturer by the name of Robert Owen set the goal of an eight-hour workday and became famous for coining the phrase, "Eight hours labor, eight hours recreation, eight hours rest."[1] What's most fascinating is that employers who started implementing the eight-hour workday found that there was no drop in productivity, and the eight-hour workday became the standard around 1919. Maybe working more doesn't necessarily mean accomplishing more.

From my work as a counselor, I can easily understand why more work doesn't necessarily lead to more success because I've seen the opposite play out time and time again. When you consider the other factors of being overworked—for example, a lack of sleep which leads to fatigue, stress, poor concentration, a lack of energy and efficiency, or even mental and physical health problems—you understand that doing more isn't the magical formula we thought it would be. Burnout is a real thing. Even high-capacity people have a capacity. And if you don't stop to find the balance, you'll eventually be forced to stop because either your body or your mind will give out on you.

Some signs you're nearing burnout could look like this: increased stress and frustration with work, people, or responsibilities; a general sense of failure and the need to "do more"; consistently feeling exhausted or fatigued; increased feelings of loneliness and isolation; lacking the energy and motivation to get things done; difficulty concentrating or engaging in sustained mental energy; increased forgetfulness; feeling a lack of accomplishment or feeling ineffective; increased feelings of anxiety or depression; increased feelings of apathy, frustration, or irritability with people around you; a lack of desire to do the things you once used to enjoy doing. Burnout is a real thing. And guess what? You can even burn out doing really good things.

Even high-capacity people have a capacity.

"CHRISTIAN" BURNOUT

I'm about to say something that might ruffle your feathers a little bit, but it's only because I care about you, and someone has to say it.

Christians struggle with burnout on a regular basis, but don't realize it because it's masked as "ministry." We blur the lines between ministry and rest and suffer greatly for it in the end. We pour out when we need to be pouring in, and we end up empty, depleted, exhausted, and sick. *But it's "Christian burnout," so that must make it okay, right?* we think. *I'm doing things for Jesus! I'm caring for people! I'm involved in ministry! I'm doing everything God has called me to do! Right?* Wrong. Because you can't continue to pour out when you reach empty. You'll have nothing left to give.

This is why building in the 8:8:8 rule in your own life is so important.

WORK

This eight-hour timeframe should be committed to whatever it is you do to make a living. For some people, that's running a business, an office job, physical labor, ministry, education, arts, or something in between. Whatever it is you do to keep food on the table and get your bills paid is considered your work. For some of you, that primary work might also include the work of being a homemaker, which is a job that (speaking from experience) can seem to never end with the many different tasks, chores, and needs. But even within the framework of running a family, it's important to try to differentiate the "work" portion (schooling, laundry, cooking, cleaning, bath, and bedtimes) from the leisure portion (game night, couch snuggles, family walks) so you don't find yourself on the brink of burnout. Consider this: How many hours per day are you "working"? There are exclusive and short-term seasons in life during which you must work overtime to make ends meet or to care for young children, and that's one thing. But consistently working more because of an unrelenting desire to have more or get more done is pushing your risk for burnout to a much higher level.

LEISURE

This is the time you spend on a combination of activities that need to be done as well as doing things that "fill you up." I like to think of my leisure time as dedicated to things that have nothing to do with my pay-the-bills work. Since my work involves mental energy (writing, counseling, creating), I like to focus on leisure activities that use physical energy (cooking up a storm, walking or hiking, being in nature, lifting weights). But if your work involves primarily using physical energy (construction, standing all day, physical labor), you might find what fills you up is something that uses mental energy (reading a book, doing something creative, picking up a long-neglected instrument, learning a new language, watching a documentary). Earlier, we talked about practicing the habit of self-care, and this is the time you would put those habits into practice.

Obviously, there must be time in our days for the necessities of daily living such as laundry, getting from one place to another, food preparation, chores, and errands. But if our leisure time ends up consistently getting spent on more output (activities of daily living) than input (self-care practices), we'll find ourselves closer and closer to burnout. When our work starts to overflow into our leisure time, the "daily life needs" or the "self-care" will get pushed down the priority ladder. And both of those are crucial to healthy living.

REST

I don't think it's a coincidence that God asked humans to prioritize rest. In fact, in Scripture we see that an entire day each week—the Sabbath—is prioritized for rest and recovery. (*Sabbath* is derived from the Hebrew word "shavat," which literally means to rest.) Jesus even reminds us that the Sabbath was made for man (Mark 2:27). It's a gift of peace, rest, and quiet in the chaos of this world. But when work spills over to leisure, leisure eventually spills over to rest—and we end up taking the time we should be sleeping and resting to check off the other things on the list that didn't get done. But rest is not optional; it's required for mental, physical, and emotional health. Our bodies need sleep to function properly. Without proper sleep, our bodies begin to shut down. Sleep affects everything from our mood, to our judgment, to our ability to learn and retain information. Not only that, but sleep deprivation has been associated with serious health risks, affecting your cardiovascular, respiratory, neurological, gastrointestinal, immune, dermatological, endocrine, and reproductive systems.

It might seem tempting to exchange a few hours of sleep each night to do something productive, but doing so regularly will eventually lead to some serious consequences. One way to prioritize sleep is by practicing an evening routine and rhythm, such as avoiding caffeine close to bedtime, sleeping and waking around the same time, limiting blue light from screen time before bed, and increasing your exposure to sunlight during the day. Following a similar bedtime routine each night is a great way to prioritize your sleep hygiene and make sure that healthy sleeping patterns are a part of your life.[2]

As you can see, time management is less about time and more about what you prioritize in your life. Make it a habit to take inventory of your work, leisure, and rest time and ask yourself what it says about your priorities. Be intentional about including times in your life to prioritize both rest and leisure. Find a healthy rhythm of Sabbath for your life, because it's the one and only way to avoid burnout.

Note: If you are dealing with symptoms of insomnia such as struggling to fall asleep, being unable to stay asleep, or finding yourself waking up much earlier than you would like for more than a two-week period, consider making an appointment with a licensed professional counselor to rule out mental health causes (such as clinical depression or anxiety) as well as meeting with a medical doctor to rule out potential physical causes and coming up with a plan to help you get the important sleep you need.

VERSE FOR REFLECTION

"The Sabbath was made for man, not man for the Sabbath" (Mark 2:27).

TODAY'S HABIT: REST

1. Take inventory of the 8:8:8 rule in your life:

   How many hours do you work?

   How many hours do you take for leisure?

   How many hours do you sleep?

2. Which of the above categories are currently out of balance in your life?

3. How do you act or react when you are lacking in rest? Do you experience mood changes, low motivation, physical energy changes, or elevated stress?

4. What is one thing you can do to prioritize rest today? What is something you can do to prioritize rest long-term?

5. Do you have one day a week that you set aside for things outside of work? What do you do during that day? If you don't have a specific day, on which day of the week could you prioritize rest?

6. Take one full day this week to practice rest and restful activities. Make note of the things that get in the way of your ability to rest and recover. (For example, getting pulled into work activities, the emails in your inbox, social media, activities of living that end up getting pushed into your rest time, or inconsistent sleep and wake times.)

INHALE AND EXHALE

BREATHE

'm about to tell you the most important thing you're doing. It's happening, right now, as your eyes are scanning the page. It's happening with or without your permission. It's happening because your body needs it to survive. You're breathing. Without your conscious awareness, your body is doing what it needs to do. It's taking in oxygen, one breath at a time, and then letting out carbon dioxide. In, and out, and in, and out. Like clockwork. Take a moment to sense what's happening, to be aware of your breathing.

The word *breath* is mentioned in the Bible numerous times. One of the very first interactions God had with man involved breathing. God breathed His breath of life into Adam (Genesis 2:7). And when Jesus appeared to the disciples after raising from the dead, "he breathed on them and said, 'Receive the Holy Spirit'" (John 20:22).

When you breathe in, air enters your nose and mouth and travels down your windpipe into your bronchial tubes, which connect to your lungs. From there, the air enters air sacs called alveoli, and passes into your bloodstream. The leftover carbon dioxide, which would be toxic to your body if it built up, then gets passed back out of your body through exhalation. Without your awareness, you're breathing 20,000 times per day. The main muscle controlling this automatic breathing is your diaphragm—tightening as you breathe in and relaxing as you breathe out.

When you feel stressed, something else automatically begins to happen. Your fight-or-flight response kicks into full gear and begins to affect your breathing. As we learned earlier, your sympathetic nervous system (your body's internal stress response alarm) starts putting different parts of your body on high alert. One of those parts is your respiratory system, and it begins to engage in quicker, shallow breaths. It's trying to get as much air as it can as quickly as it can. But ironically, the opposite happens.

Have you ever noticed your breathing change in times of anxiety or stress? Some people feel like their breath becomes so shallow they can hardly breathe. Another word for this is *hyperventilating*, which means *over*breathing. You're actually breathing too much. This can cause you to feel dizzy and lightheaded, dry your mouth, create a feeling of tingling in your body, or cause your heart rate to spike. These physical reactions can happen frequently when someone is struggling with anxiety and panic.

I experienced all these symptoms the very first time I had a panic attack. I literally felt like my body was going to shut down. My mind was spiraling out of control, and in response, so was my body. I was sweating, dizzy, lightheaded, and weak. My mouth felt parched, and I began to feel a tingling sensation starting from the tips of my fingers all the way up my arms and to my face. *This is it*, I thought. *I'm about to die*. When really, controlling my breathing could have brought me much-needed relief.

FIGHT PHYSICAL WITH PHYSICAL

Even though our breathing is automatic, we can still override the default stress response and take back control. Even while our sympathetic system is on high-alert mode, we can practice controlled breathing exercises to get our body back to baseline. In my counseling office, I've practiced breathing exercises with many of my clients as part of helping them alleviate the physical symptoms of anxiety. "We'll fight physical with physical," I tell them. And when our body is back to baseline, we can fight "mental with mental." What I mean by that is when your body feels so stressed that it feels like it's going to shut down, giving yourself a logical pep talk isn't going to be of much help in the moment.

Your amygdala (the part of your brain that responds to stress and puts your body into fight-or-flight mode), isn't checking in with your cortex (the part of your brain that processes logical thinking) during times of panic, anxiety, and stress. It's just responding to stress cues. And that's a good thing, because sometimes you need your amygdala to respond without wasting time checking in! For example, if a truck is coming at you at 70 miles per hour as you're crossing the street, your fight-or-flight response will be what gets you to jump out of the way. Thank God it's not taking the time to check in with your logical side: "Hey, see that truck coming? Looks like it's going fast. What do you think we should do?" Because you'd be a dead person in a split second. The amygdala is recognizing stress cues and responding instantaneously, leaving the logical part of your brain in the dust. At least for the time being.

This is why we have to learn to fight physical with physical. And later, when our cortex is back in the game, we can fight mental with mental, using some of the cognitive thought replacing and reframing habits mentioned throughout this book. Breathing exercises are specifically designed to get your body back to baseline.

> There is power in your breath, and most importantly,
> in the God who gave you that breath.

BREATHING EXERCISES

If you're in the therapy and counseling world long enough, you'll eventually hear about a practice called *mindfulness*. Mindfulness is another word for meditation, the discipline of being aware—aware of what's going on inside of you as well as what's going on around you. In counseling, the practice of meditation and mindfulness is paired with important breathing exercises. The Bible encourages us to "meditate" on good things, such as truth, and God's Word, and things that are good and beneficial (Isaiah 26:3; Joshua 1:8; Philippians 4:8). Mindfulness causes your body and mind to slow down, and in turn, allows your sympathetic system to get back to baseline. Implementing mindfulness strategies has been scientifically proven to significantly reduce symptoms of anxiety, panic, and depression.[1]

How you breathe and your awareness of your breath has the ability to reduce your stress. But let me reiterate—it doesn't "delete" your stress. When your body is back to baseline there will be more work to do internally (getting to the root causes of stress, understanding the underlying thoughts that cause stress, learning to respond to your feelings accordingly). But there are times you need to fight physical with physical. I want you to have this tool in your toolbox for those times. I want you to know that you have the power to reset your body, or even prevent it from getting worked up in the first place.

When you've recognized the "false alarms" in your life that we talked about earlier, you can begin implementing mindfulness and breathing exercises to help your body stay steady. There are thousands of mindfulness exercises out there, but one of my favorites pairs the truth of Scripture with the power of breathing exercises. This is what we'll be doing in today's practice. I want you to practice this exercise long before you need it—don't wait until you're overly stressed to try it. I want it to become a regular habit that you go back to again and again to begin learning how to regularly tune in to what's going on inside of you as well as around you.

There is power in your breath, and most importantly, in the God who gave you that breath. Just as He fills your lungs with air, may He fill your life with peace. With every breath you breathe, praise Him. Inhale, exhale. Praise the Lord.

VERSE FOR REFLECTION

"Let everything that has breath praise the LORD!" (Psalm 150:6).

TODAY'S HABIT: BREATHE

Before we begin today's exercise, consider the difference between chest breathing and diaphragm breathing. Diaphragm breathing is the deep breathing that moves your stomach in and out (because when you breathe deeply, your diaphragm contracts down toward your stomach). This breathing is what will help you override your stress response and get your body back to baseline. Chest breathing is the shallow breathing that you only feel in your upper chest because you're not taking in enough air to expand your lower lungs. Chest breathing may move your shoulders up and down, while diaphragm breathing should move your belly in and out. Take a few minutes to deeply breathe in and out, and see if you can breathe in a way that moves your stomach in and out. That is diaphragm breathing. Once you've gotten the hang of it, let's move to today's activity.

A great resource on the practice of mindfulness and meditation is a book called *Holy Noticing* by Charles Stone. Not only does he lay out the biblical and scientific foundations for the practice of mindfulness, but he also offers a practical method of engaging in mindfulness. In his book, he describes what he calls the BREATHe method, going through each of the letters of the word *breathe*.

> **B:** Body—being aware of your physical body states and sensations as well as controlling your breathing. (You will focus specifically on this one today, and when you're ready for deeper mindfulness you can move on to the others as well.)
>
> **R:** Relationships—assessing the health of your relationships.
>
> **E:** Environment—taking notice of your current surroundings including sights, sounds, smells, and God's creation.
>
> **A:** Afflictive emotions or Affect—acknowledging how you're currently feeling.
>
> **T:** Thoughts—being conscious of your current thoughts.

H: Heart—paying attention to the state of your spiritual life and Holy Spirit's whisperings or impressions on your heart.

e: engage—engaging the world like Christ, practicing holy noticing in the mundane, the everyday, the ordinary. [2]

The act of mindfulness is essentially taking a "scan" of your entire body, from the inside out, from the top to bottom, stopping to pay special attention to areas of struggle. Today, we're going to place our focus on controlling our breathing. When I'm walking my clients through a traditional mindfulness exercise, I always make sure we begin by closing our eyes as a method of focus, and then paying extra attention to our breathing patterns as we begin to tune into the physical components of the body. *Inhale—exhale. Inhale—exhale.* It can often help to keep your mouth slightly pursed as you breathe in and breathe out. Now slowly breathe in, counting to five, and then slowly breathe out, again on a five-count. Incorporating Scripture during this time can mean taking any verse or phrase from God's Word that is meaningful to you and integrating it into your time of breathing. In *Holy Noticing*, Charles Stone recommends mentally using the phrase "Holy Spirit" on your breath in and "breathe on me," on your breath out.[3] Repeat this over and over in your mind until you have a consistently slow, controlled breathing pattern.

The next step in the practice of mindfulness is to take inventory of your body regarding your muscles. From the top of your head to the bottom of your toes, with your eyes still closed, you allow your focus to spotlight every muscle and take inventory of any tension you might be carrying in your body. Don't let your mind wander to the things that might be causing stress, but keep your mind focused on each part of your body as you continue to inhale and exhale.

In *Holy Noticing*, Stone urges us not to simply take note of our muscle tension as we scan through each body part, but to then go the next step and thank God for that part of our body, ending with this simple prayer: *Lord, thank You for giving me my body. I am fearfully and wonderfully made. I yield it to You today as a living sacrifice.*[4] This simple prayer also helps keep your mind from wandering and focuses it inward.

Once you've controlled your breathing and relaxed your muscles (you've fought physical with physical), it's time to take inventory from the inside out (to fight mental with mental). It's time to notice. This is where the BREATHe method of mindfulness mentioned above can be especially helpful, and I highly recommend you take the time to read through the entire book as you develop the art of mindfulness as a regular practice in your life. But please remember, it might take some time to learn how to focus on the physical components of mindfulness first (the letter B in the BREATHe method) and you may need to go back to it again and again before you're ready to move on to the other steps in the BREATHe method. But if nothing else, remember this: *Inhale. Exhale. Praise the Lord.*

KNOW YOUR ENEMIES

IDENTIFY THE OBSTACLES

I f you sat down with me for a counseling session, one of the things you'd learn is that when it comes to making changes in your life, you've got to know your enemies and understand your obstacles. What is holding you back? What are the barriers that get in the way of your action plan to change? When it's finally time to make the changes and put into practice what you want to do, what stops you? When do you fail? Why do you fail? Understanding the answers to these questions is a huge part of learning how to stop getting stuck.

I worked with a young man who wanted to break free of his struggle with porn. He had the will to change—a genuine, deep desire to change—but ended up falling back into porn use again and again. He would beat himself up about it, confess to his wife, and then try again. One of those three things is the counterproductive thing to do. Can you guess which one?

Beating yourself up will inevitably dig you into a pit of shame. Instead of seeing his mistakes as an opportunity to evaluate and readjust, he ruminated about his mistakes, felt miserable about himself, and ended up falling right back into the unhealthy habit. Feeling shame increases our tendency to make bad decisions because we end up punishing ourselves. We feel so guilty that we end up defaulting back to unhealthy behaviors in an attempt to cope with those uncomfortable feelings of guilt and shame. Responding to your relapse, mistakes, or failures with shame will escort you right back into the very cycle you're trying to break. Shame digs the hole deeper, but grace lifts us out of the hole. Grace for yourself doesn't mean you pretend like nothing happened. It means you care for God, yourself, and others enough to get back up and try again.

My client had to start by seeing his relapse as a learning opportunity. What could he learn from his mistake? I asked him to map out his day for me, from start to finish, and talk me through the times he struggled the most. We identified a few things that got in the way of his desire for freedom: underlying stress, excess alone time, and fatigue. Like clockwork, the three times he had a higher tendency to fall back into porn was when he was feeling overly stressed, had too much alone time, or was feeling extra tired. We tracked his schedule for a few weeks and the same patterns came up again and again. Now he was starting to recognize his enemies—the obstacles that were holding him back. We came up with boundaries and barriers to help protect him during those vulnerable times as well as a plan to help him deal with the root emotions and underlying stress, and little by little, he started moving into victory.

Shame digs the hole deeper, but grace lifts us out of the hole.

THE CYCLE OF HEALING

You've got to do the same thing. You've got to shift your thinking. Instead of seeing your mistakes as "relapses," lean into them as lessons—lessons to help you get to the root and understand your obstacles. Because you can either beat yourself up over a mistake and then continue to let it happen, or you can learn from it—readjust, make some changes, and try again.

Healing is not linear. You don't just get better and better each day.

Healing is cyclical—a few steps forward, followed by a couple steps back, followed by a few more steps forward. It's a pattern of trying, failing, and trying again. And with each trial we get a little stronger, a little steadier, and a little more healed. You can either choose to engage in the cycle of shame or the cycle of healing.

With that in mind, let's take some time to analyze your mistakes and setbacks. Take a moment to think about something you've wanted to change or an area you've wanted to grow. Next, try to pinpoint the times when you've failed. What were your obstacles?

The successful 12-step recovery group Alcoholics Anonymous teaches an acronym to help people know their enemies. They call it HALT because it reminds you to stop and consider your obstacles. HALT stands for a few of the most common enemies you need to be aware of from day to day. Let's talk through what each letter means.

(H) Hungry

If you're anything like me, you know that hunger makes you susceptible to irritability, mood swings, and an overall tendency toward bad decisions. So much that we've coined the terms *hangry* and *food swings*. Low blood sugar levels impact your serotonin, which impacts your ability to think rationally and stick to your goals. In other words, there's a scientific reason hunger can become an obstacle. Don't allow yourself to get to the point where you're starving, angry, and irritable. Stay ahead of it by fueling your body.

It's not just about filling yourself up, either—it's about learning to fuel yourself with healthy and nutritious foods. Recent scientific evidence is making a clear case for a connection to our nutritional health and our mental and emotional health. So don't just fill your body with fats, sugars, and simple carbs. Fuel it with healthy proteins, fruits, vegetables, and whole grains. The other thing I'll add to this category is proper hydration! Don't let yourself get hungry *or* thirsty. Drink the recommended eight eight-ounce glasses of water per day. It makes a bigger difference than you realize with your physical stamina. My friend Levi Lusko said it like this: "You might not have a demon, you might just be dehydrated!"[1] The bottom line is this: Keep yourself stable physically so you have a better chance of staying stable mentally, emotionally, and behaviorally.

(A) Angry

I always say that anger is a secondary emotion because it usually reveals something deeper going on underneath the surface. Anger just happens to be the easiest emotion to express because it's packed with emotional force, so it pours out of us when emotions run high. And because of the impulsivity that often accompanies anger, you're likely to make decisions you'll regret in hindsight. Anger suppresses your ability to think clearly (because of the amygdala response we talked about earlier) and sends your body into fight-or-flight mode. In this case, it's usually "fight."

Underneath that anger, there's more. Underneath anger, there are other emotions that require more processing, insight, and vulnerability to understand and express. You could be angry on the outside, but what you're really feeling deep down is fear, hurt, insecurity, or shame. You could be angry on the outside but what you're really feeling is misunderstood, unwanted, or inadequate. You could be angry on the outside but what you're really feeling is stress, anxiety, and worry. Or depression, discouragement, and disillusionment. Remember the obstacle of anger and keep yourself away from making impulsive decisions until your anger and strong emotions have subsided. We'll talk about some ways to do that in today's activity.

(L) Lonely

When you feel extreme loneliness, you start to question if there's anyone who cares. You feel like you're lacking in support and concern from others, and you start to feel desperate. And when you feel desperate, you make desperate decisions. Usually, it's in those times that you are most susceptible to turning to unhealthy things to fill the void of loneliness. Some people find themselves defaulting to obsessive time on social media, unhealthy dating relationships, emotional or physical affairs, substances like drugs and alcohol, pornography, shopping or gambling—anything to fill the void of loneliness. This is why it's so important to make sure you're prepared for this obstacle when it comes and to surround yourself with barriers to protect yourself from getting to this place. But most importantly, remember that you're never really alone. Earlier we talked about what it looks like to shift our isolation into solitude and lean into God's faithful presence even in the times we feel the most alone. This is when that shift matters the most.

(T) Tired

When you're tired, even nominal tasks can seem overwhelming. We talked previously about how sleep can impact our physical and emotional health, but a lack of sleep can also impact our moral judgment and decision-making. One study took 26 individuals and asked them to make judgment calls about different moral dilemmas they were presented with at two separate times: when they were well rested versus after two nights without sleep.[2] When sleep-deprived, it took them significantly longer to decide whether an action was morally appropriate. The internal judgment of their sleep-deprived selves was lagging in comparison to their well-rested selves. The study suggests that you're much more likely to make better, faster, more confident decisions when you're well rested. You're much more likely to distinguish healthy choices from unhealthy choices when you've had enough sleep. This is why it's important to understand this obstacle and prioritize giving your body the rest that it needs.

There are three more letters I want to add to the HALT acronym—obstacles I've observed that keep people stuck.

(S) Sick

When you're not feeling physically well, you're more prone to making decisions you wouldn't otherwise make. This isn't exclusive to severe physical illness, either, but also includes something as common as a headache, a cold or virus, or not feeling well due to hormones during that time of the month. It could be joint pain, or muscle aches, or a sinus infection. The key is remembering that during times you're phys-ically down, it's easy to also become emotionally down and fall into a behavior or decision you wouldn't otherwise. Be in tune to how you feel and surround yourself with protective barriers during vulnerable times so you don't get stuck.

(B) Bored

This is an underappreciated reason why so many of us fail. One study showed that teens who were bored were more likely to engage in binge drinking, had fewer hobbies, and were more at risk for internet addiction. And I know boredom isn't just a vice for teenagers, because boredom has sabotaged my own desires for healthy eating—for exam-ple, those nights when I'm feeling bored (not actually hungry) and just want something to munch on, sugar in the pantry seems much more tempting than it would if I were occupied. Sometimes in our boredom, we find something to do to kill time that ends up harming us more than helping us. Get in front of boredom. Map out your day and be in tune to the times when you've felt the most bored and how that has affected your decision-making.

(R) Reward

The last obstacle I'll add is a little different from the previous ones, because this is when we use a negative or harmful behavior as a "reward." Maybe we've had a hard day and are looking for something to cheer us up, or we want to pat ourselves on the back for an accomplishment or success. We can self-sabotage by rewarding ourselves with something that ends up harming us in the end. Our brain is driven and motivated by rewards, and when it gets one, it wants more of it. It's like giving yourself a big glass of wine at the end of a long week when you're trying to quit alcohol. Or sitting down with a big tub of Ben and Jerry's after a few days of healthy eating, when you're trying to drop some weight. In the end, you've actually set yourself up to struggle more the next time because now your brain is searching for that reward. This is when it's important to see that the *real* reward is changed behavior. There's a reason you want it. So don't give up now. Set up some healthy rewards along the way to help you get there (a warm bath instead of that glass of wine, a big bowl of berries and a piece of dark chocolate instead of that tub of Ben and Jerry's).

To win the battle, you need to know your enemies. And often they don't appear to be as scary and obvious as you'd imagine. But that's what makes them so dangerous—they're enemies that easily blend into your day-to-day life. Know what they are and be on the lookout. Choose to let go of the cycle of shame and instead engage in the cycle of healing.

VERSE FOR REFLECTION

"There is now no condemnation for those who are in Christ Jesus" (Romans 8:1).

TODAY'S HABIT: IDENTIFY THE OBSTACLES

1. Take a few moments to map out your day, particularly making note of the time of day you struggle the most with an unwanted behavior, decision, actions, or interactions. What did you observe? Which times are you more vulnerable to certain obstacles?

2. Which of the obstacles listed tend to sabotage your growth and goals?

3. On a separate sheet of paper write out the acronym, HALT SBR. Take a moment to write down an action plan for each letter, focusing especially on the ones you struggle with the most. What can you do to protect yourself during those vulnerable times? See examples below, and then write your own.

Hungry: *Bring a snack with me, eat before I go, don't let more than three hours go by without a healthy snack, fill up with nutritious foods.*

Angry: *Talk to someone about my feelings, write in my journal when I'm feeling something deeply, take a walk outside to process my feelings, work with a counselor to discover underlying emotions.*

Lonely: *Call a friend and ask for prayer, meet someone for coffee, FaceTime to catch up with a family member, spend some time on a prayer walk and connect with God, plan ahead for regular get-togethers.*

Tired: *Be intentional with sleep hygiene, take a 20-minute power nap, take a quick run or walk to increase energy levels.*

Sick: *Make myself comfortable with a heating pad or a warm bath, ask for help and support from others.*

Bored: *Plan a spontaneous outing with a friend, read a book, have a project that I only work on in my down time, take the time to do something creative.*

Reward: *Set up healthy reward such as nutritious food, a special outing with a friend or loved one, or a vacation to look forward to.*

STAY ATTACHED

CONNECT WITH GOD AND OTHERS

Human beings are magnetic.

We tend to attract and engage with people who are similar to us in appearance and style. Studies have even shown that we're more likely to be drawn to people who resemble either ourselves or our parents.[1] We tend to choose what is familiar over what is healthy. If that applies to the physical realm, how much more might this familiarity affect us on the emotional and relational level? According to attachment theory, more than we realize.

Attachment theory is a counseling principle that refers to our ability to connect with our emotions as well as significant others in our lives. The two go hand in hand, because how we interact and express our emotions is a big part of how we engage with others. According to attachment theory, there are two main types of attachment: secure or insecure. Secure attachment refers to a healthy connection with others: *I know you're here for me, and I'm here for you.* Insecure attachment means we struggle to feel consistently wanted, loved, valued, needed, appreciated, or cared for. And no matter how secure we feel, deep down, each of us struggles with a little insecurity (sometimes a lot) in our relationships from time to time. We all have a little bit of insecure attachment inside us, and recognizing how our attachment style plays out will help us connect with God and others in a deeper and more meaningful way. So let's dig a little deeper. When it comes to insecure attachment, there are three broad types.[2]

ANXIOUS ATTACHMENT

Anxious attachment means you're often worried about and deeply aware of your relationships with others. The deep questions in your mind are: *Do you really care enough about me? Are you really there for me?* You have a desperate desire for closeness and want to cultivate an environment where you feel connected to the people around you. When they pull away, you give more to try to bridge the gap. If they're distant, you desperately try to make the situation better. Because of this, you can sometimes find yourself in one-sided relationships where you're doing much of the work. You might also find yourself coming across as needy or clingy. Because you desperately seek an emotional connection with others, you're comfortable displaying emotions that sometimes others are not comfortable with.

People with anxious attachment style may come from a background of instability where they had to "fix" the relationships around them or "keep everyone together," or where they were responsible to fill in the emotional gaps of their own unmet needs. Anxious attachment means you put much of the responsibility of maintaining close relationships on your own shoulders. You carry the false belief that if you stop trying, and working, and connecting, the relationship may not make it.

SHUT-DOWN ATTACHMENT

Shut-down attachment style means you're more comfortable relying on yourself. In fact, you prefer to have control, where you don't have to rely on others for your needs. What you're really feeling deep down is: *People can't be trusted, so I have to take care of myself. In order to maintain relationships, it's better to keep feelings in and deal with things on my own.* Because of this, you tend to keep people at a distance emotionally and keep your own emotions at a distance as well. In essence, you learn to "shut down" a certain side of you as a form of self-protection.

People who struggle with a shut-down attachment style may have a past where emotions were not allowed to be shown. "You'd better stop crying or I'll give you something to cry about," might have been a theme in your childhood. Or maybe you grew up in a family where being logical was better than emotional, so you stuffed your feelings and used your head instead. Or maybe your emotional needs were never met because of caregivers who were too wrapped up or distracted in their own world, and so you respond by learning to care for yourself and believing that you don't really need others. Whatever the situation, when you live in a shut-down way, you tend to keep people at a distance rather than bringing them close.

SHAME-BASED ATTACHMENT

Shame-filled attachment means that you tend to blame yourself for your relationship failures. You might critique, guilt, and shame yourself as you try harder and harder to get better. You might even feel like you don't "deserve" relationships or that you're "not good enough" for love and intimacy. You spend your life trying to prove to others that you are worth loving, but deep down you struggle with the thought, *Am I actually worthy of love? If they only knew the real me, they would leave.* So even though you desire intimate relationships, you tend to push others away out of fear that they'll get a glimpse of "the real you" and run away.

People who struggle with this type of attachment may come from a background where there was abuse or violence. Shame was put on you, so you continue to carry that shame. You might come from a background where there was inconsistency with how you were loved: one day you were praised, and the next you were mistreated. You assume that the way people treat you has something to do with who you are or how you're behaving and put all the pressure on yourself. If only you were good enough, smart enough, behaved enough. At the end of the day, you keep people away out of fear that you'll be exposed.

You might see yourself in one or even a little of all these attachment styles. Understanding the way we attach, and why, can help us heal. Instead of defaulting to our insecure attachment style, we can dig a little deeper and figure out what's going on underneath the surface. We can choose to respond to the people around us in healthy ways rather than unhealthy ways.

We tend to choose what is familiar over what is healthy.

OUR ATTACHMENT TO GOD

I've always said that our spiritual health has less to do with what we do for God (the spiritual checklist of reading the Bible, praying, church, ministry) and more to do with how we see and experience God. From my work with clients as well as in my personal life, I see so clearly that the wounds of our past will shape our view of God. The way we've been treated by others can often influence the way we view God. The young man who grew up in a home full of criticism and critique, feeling like he was never good enough, may view God as condemning and critical of his every move. The girl who lived with an apathetic mother may grow up to view God as far away, distant, and uninterested in her life.

Just as we tend to view God through the lens of our past, we also tend to "attach" to God based on our attachment styles. In the book *Attached to God*, the author outlines our tendency to feel an insecure attachment in our relationship with God based on our personal attachment style.[3]

- Maybe we're worried and anxious that God won't stay close, so we desperately try to keep Him near using our daily spiritual checklist. We have to continuously do our part so God will stay.

- Maybe we're shut down, afraid to show Him our feelings because we don't want Him to be disappointed in us. So we go through the motions of faith without ever allowing ourselves to feel.

- Maybe we're filled with shame, wondering if we're even good enough for God. We blame ourselves when things don't go right and assume God doesn't love us as much as He loves everyone else.

I don't know if you can relate to any of these, but I do know this: God wants us to stay close (John 15:4). He has created us to attach to others as well as to Himself. He's longing for us to attach to Him and stay attached to Him. To remain in Him.

Whatever we have is not "too much" for Him to handle. Maybe you've been told by others that your emotions are too big. That your past is too complicated. That your mistakes are too many. That your flaws are too obvious. That your drama is too overwhelming. That your personality is too much. But let me assure you, God's container can hold everything you have to pour out and so much more.

He can handle you. And not only *can* He handle you, He *wants* to. He wants everything you have to offer. He wants you to come close, to draw near, and to give it all to Him. Nothing you have will be too overwhelming. Not your past, not your emotions, not your personality, not your drama. Nothing. You don't have to hold back in His presence. You don't have to try to keep it all together. You don't even have to prove yourself. You're invited to come, to get near, and to stay close. You're invited to attach.

God wants us to stay close. He has created us
to attach to others as well as to Himself.

STAY ATTACHED

I want you to take a moment to reflect on your relationships with God and with others. I want you to tune in to your tendency to pull away or desperately try to draw near in fear that God will pull away.

We were created for relationship by a God who made us to be in relationship with Him. But sometimes our own insecurities keep us from staying attached to God and others. I could give you a list of activities to participate in, events to attend, and checklists to complete, but for now I want you to forget those external things and instead consider the things deep inside you—the insecurities, faulty beliefs, and fears—that might keep you from securely connecting with both God and others; from truly believing that there's a special place for you with God and with His people.

We were made for relationships. And we become the healthiest versions of ourselves when we can heal from our past hurts and learn to stay attached. Attached to God and attached to others.

VERSE FOR REFLECTION

"Remain in me, as I also remain in you. No branch can bear fruit by itself; it must remain in the vine. Neither can you bear fruit unless you remain in me" (John 15:4).

TODAY'S HABIT: CONNECT WITH GOD AND OTHERS

1. Out of the three insecure attachment styles listed, which one do you relate with the most?

2. List some experiences from your past that may have influenced your attachment style.

3. How does your attachment style play out in your relationship with others? How does it play out in your relationship with God?

4. What is one thing you can do this week to intentionally stay attached to God?

5. What is one thing you can do this week to intentionally stay attached to others?

DISTRACTIONS ALL AROUND

STAY FOCUSED

By now I hope you've started to notice that distractions are all around you.

There's probably something distracting you even as you're reading this page. It could be the phone in your pocket, its muffled ding alerting you to a new text message. Or maybe it's that notification that popped up on your screen while you're trying to read, letting you know about an email or DM in your inbox, or beckoning you to read that new message you just received on social media. Maybe your dog is barking in the background, your kids are playing nearby, or you hear noises outside your window. It could be that your TV is on in the background, competing for your attention.

As one writer puts it, "On average, we experience an interruption every eight minutes or about seven or eight per hour. In an eight-hour day, that is about 60 interruptions. The average interruption takes about five minutes, so that is about five hours out of eight. And if it takes around 15 minutes to resume the interrupted activity at a good level of concentration, this means that we are never concentrating very well."[1] Not only that, but one study reported that people check their phone every 12 minutes during their waking hours. Seventy-one percent of people said they never turn their phone off, and 40 percent said they check their phone within five minutes of waking up.[2] Add to that the distractions of everyday life, and you'll see clearly that we have a lot competing for our attention. And here's why this matters: Focus is the space in which change begins to happen.

A few lessons ago, we talked about the importance of unplugging and withdrawing, of being deliberate to connect with God in the midst of all the distractions competing for our time. But today I want to shift your attention to another form of distraction we're competing with that's become very commonplace and even celebrated in our culture: busyness.

"I've been busy!" That's the phrase I hear most often when I ask people how they've been. And what's interesting is that we say it as though it's a badge of honor to be busy. As though being busy means you are more important, or valuable, or desired, or necessary than everyone else around you. But what if it was actually the opposite? What if, in being so "busy," we weren't just doing more—we were experiencing less? What if, in the hustle and bustle and fast pace of life, we were missing something—namely, what's happening right in front of us, what's happening deep within us? What if we were losing our ability to focus, to feel, to fill up?

Focus is the space in which change begins to happen.

THE CONSEQUENCE OF MORE

There's something I need you to hear: *Sometimes, we do more to feel less.*

More plans, more screen time, more Netflix, more emails, more activities, more sports, more podcasts. Distraction, busyness, and rush are some of the best ways to keep ourselves from feeling and experiencing the here and now, the best ways to shift our attention elsewhere.

And maybe we're not doing it on purpose, not consciously trying to tune out what's going on in front of us and inside us. But by engaging in the fast pace of the external, we're unable to keep up with the internal. *When you do more, you feel less.* Not only does staying busy prevent us from tuning into our feelings, but it also distracts us from being aware of how we're really doing on the inside.

Jesus reminds us to slow down and tune in. To stop, and sit, and look inward, and learn. To be present. Right here and right now. You don't need to look too far into Scripture to realize that distraction is nothing new. Go to the story of Martha and Mary, and you'll find that distraction existed long before iPhones, emails, and text alerts. Martha was distracted, there was so much going on, so much to do. But she was so caught up in everything going on around her that she missed what was right in front of her: Jesus.

Right here, right now, she had the opportunity to connect with the face of God, to tune in to His presence and be filled up. Right here and right now, she had everything she needed. But she was missing it because she was distracted (Luke 10:40).

I feel for Martha. Maybe because I'm a little more like Martha than I am Mary. I thrive on multitasking, being efficient, thinking forward, and getting as much done as I can. The Marys of this world just don't speak my language. They're just so chill, calm, present, and laid-back. But here's the beautiful thing about this story: Choosing a different personality type isn't the answer to all our problems. It's about choosing a *person.* It's about choosing to be present with Jesus. Wherever He is, that's where I want to be. Whatever He's doing, that's what I want to be a part of. And so many times, in my busyness and distraction and my desire to get things done *for* Him, I *miss* Him. I miss what He's doing, saying, and teaching. I get off track and off focus and tune in more to what's going on around me than to what's going on in front of me and inside me.

By this point in the book, whatever it is you had in mind to work on, grow in, or change could have easily gotten missed in the many distractions life has thrown at you along the way. But this is my encouragement for you to recalibrate and stay focused. Stay present. Continue clearing out the internal noise and clutter from your life and make space for change. Make space to lean in, learn, and heal. Make space for Jesus to do what He's going to do.

> ## VERSE FOR REFLECTION
>
> "Martha was distracted by all the preparations that had to be made" (Luke 10:40).

TODAY'S HABIT: STAY FOCUSED

1. Write down three main distractions that come up in your life on a regular basis. How do those distractions get in the way of your progress? Next to each distraction, write down one way you can alleviate, minimize, or avoid the distraction.

2. "When we do more, we feel less." Take a look at your life's pace and schedule and ask yourself if you're making space for healing. If so, what does that look like? If not, what can you do to begin making space?

3. Rewrite the one thing you had in mind to grow, change, or heal at the beginning of the book. How have you stayed focused on that portion of your life? How have you gotten distracted from that goal?

4. Take some time to be deliberately present today. Put aside distractions and tune in to what's going on inside you. Savor the details of what's happening in the here and now with the people you love and the God you love. Tune in to the sights, sounds, smells, and experiences. Capture the details of your life right here and right now. And look for God in it.

CONCENTRATE AND ELIMINATE

SET HEALTHY BOUNDARIES

T he trend of minimalism is sweeping the nation—getting rid of your excess so you can focus on enjoying the things that add value and meaning to your life. Most of the time when we talk about minimalism, we're talking about the excess physical things in our world—the clothes, the toys, the kitchen appliances, the books, the electronics...all the *stuff*. But what if we could also apply that concept to other areas of our lives?

Years before the concept of minimalism became so popular, I read a book in which the author, Anne Ortlund, talked about the importance of focusing on the essentials. She coined the phrase "concentrate and eliminate" and applied that strategy to everything from her closet to her schedule.[1] That concept has resonated with me ever since, and I've been intentionally trying to use that idea as a framework for my life. Concentrate on what's important, eliminate the excess. Concentrate on the essentials, eliminate the extras. Concentrate on the majors, eliminate the minors. Essentially, this is the art of setting boundaries.

Setting boundaries is a big theme in my life. Learning when to say yes and when to say no is essential to becoming healthy people.

It's essential to changing our lives. I teach about boundaries in some way, shape, or form in every single one of my books. In fact, the word *boundaries* has already come up over a dozen times in this book alone. I really believe that boundaries protect us, protect our relationships, and protect our God-given calling. Boundaries are the line we draw around our lives, keeping the valuable and meaningful things in and the distractions and excess out.

In our last habit we talked about the struggle of distraction and how important it is to stay focused. Boundaries are the practical next steps to dealing with our distraction. When Jesus saw how distracted Martha was, He responded to her with affirmation that, yes, there are so many distractions, so many things that can get in our way. But He took it a little further. Once we recognize the distractions, we do something about them. There are "many things, but few things are needed," He gently reminded her (Luke 10:41-42). Concentrate on what is needed—on what matters the most. Set a boundary in your life, draw a line in the sand, and commit to focusing on the essentials.

THE MOST IMPORTANT THINGS

You're given a pile of rocks, some pebbles, and a pile of sand and asked to fill an empty jar. How you complete this task matters. If you first fill the jar with the sand, followed by the pebbles, followed by the rocks, the materials won't all fit. The jar can't hold them. But if you put in the rocks first, followed by the pebbles, you can pour in the sand last and it will fill in all the extra crevices. The order matters.[2]

Business leaders, pastors, and teachers alike use this illustration as a challenge to focus on our priorities and boundaries. Essentially, the big rocks symbolize the things that matter most to you in life: your relationship with God, your family and friendships, and your personal health (mental, emotional, spiritual, physical). The pebbles symbolize the things of secondary importance: your work, ministry, education, and activities of daily living. The pile of sand symbolizes the things of little importance—the minors in your life that take up time and space ("to-dos," meetings, extra activities). You can also look at these three items in terms of consequences. The rocks are the things that will have serious negative consequences if left neglected. The pebbles are the things that will have moderate consequences if left neglected. And the sand stands for things that will have minor consequences if left neglected.

The problem is, we often get these three piles confused. We tend to focus too much on the minors and neglect the majors. Sometimes, the pile of sand ends up getting more of our attention, and in the end, we have no room for the rocks. When our boundaries and priorities get out of sync, so does our life.

THE ROOTS OF YES

One of the ways we get our priorities back in check is by learning to say no. *No* is the magic word that keeps our priorities intact and our lives decluttered. *No* helps us realize that some things are essential and other things aren't. *No* helps us place value on the things that add meaning to our lives and the things God has called us to and clear away the things that distract us. *No* helps us put the rocks, pebbles, and sand of our lives in just the right order.

But if it were as easy as simply saying no more, most of us would have the boundaries thing down. There's more to it than that. For us to learn how to say no, we've got to get to the roots of why we say yes to begin with. What is happening underneath the surface that motivates us to do more, agree to more, schedule more, buy more, accomplish more, commit to more?

Maybe underneath the surface we're driven by the false belief that to do more means to be more. We put our value in what we do, so we continue to do, and do, and do, until we can't do anymore.

Maybe we're driven by feelings of guilt and obligation, feeling like we owe it to the world to say yes and to be there for everyone's needs.

Maybe we're afraid of letting people down, wanting so badly to be loved, needed, and wanted that we'll do whatever it takes to show people we're worth keeping close.

Maybe we're under the false impression that we need to be the ones to fix everything, to step in and be the heroes, the peacemakers, and the first responders to every broken or difficult situation. If we don't do it, who will?

Whatever it is, when you can get to the root of your yes and correct it with God's truth, you'll find that saying no becomes a lot easier. Setting boundaries becomes attainable.

ELIMINATE THE EXCESS

Sometimes we need to purge things from our lives to make room for the things that matter most. We're distracted by too many things, and instead we need to focus on just a few things. What does it look like for you to concentrate and eliminate the excess in this season? If your plate feels too full, there's a good chance it is. If you're consistently piling more, and more, and more things on your plate without taking anything off, eventually the plate will break. It's basic mechanics, but it certainly applies to emotional and mental health as well. Some of you are in a serious season of struggle right now, yet there's a simple solution: Take some things off your plate. Refuse to believe the lie that everything is essential. Refuse to believe the lie that you need to be the one to fix it, to accomplish it, and to get it done. Refuse to believe the lie that tells you that your value comes from what you do and what you accomplish. Free yourself from those heavy burdens and focus on the few essential things God has called you to, the "few things" that are needed. Because if your plate breaks, it takes everything with it.

What if we could own our thoughts, understand our emotions, and change our lives long before we get to the point where it's life or death? What if we could remain in a healthy place and actually stay there? How would that impact our lives, our families, our calling?

I don't know how close you feel to your breaking point right now, but I do know this: We weren't made to live desperately in this life; we were made to live abundantly (John 10:10). Jesus comes to give life abundant, and the enemy comes to steal it away. When you're simply surviving and not thriving, that's not God. It's the enemy. When you're feeling burnt out, empty, and depleted—that's not God, it's the enemy. When you're stuck in a cycle of shame and unhealthy habits—that's not God, it's the enemy. When your plate feels so full it's about to break—that's not God, it's the enemy. We've got to tune in to what's going on and learn to care for ourselves before we shut down and burn out. We've got to throw off everything that hinders and entangles us so we can finish the race God has called us to run with power, strength, and dignity (Hebrews 12:1). We've got to fix our eyes on Jesus so we can finish well.

Like Mary, what does it look like to choose "what is better" in this season of your life? What does it look like to focus on the essentials? What does it look like to *reset* the way you've always done things and start to do them differently? What does it look like to slow down and make space for God to do a work in your life? What does it look like to sit at the feet of Jesus and let Him pour into you? Because only one thing is needed. And it's Jesus. Let's never forget it.

VERSE FOR REFLECTION

"Martha, Martha," the Lord answered, "you are worried and upset about many things, but few things are needed—or indeed only one. Mary has chosen what is better, and it will not be taken away from her" (Luke 10:41-42).

TODAY'S HABIT: SET HEALTHY BOUNDARIES

1. List the things that fall into the following categories in your own life:

   Rocks (the essentials)

   Pebbles (the important)

   Sand (the extras)

2. How has a lack of prioritizing affected your life in a negative way? What important things end up suffering when your priorities get out of sync?

3. What does it look like to eliminate the excess from your life and schedule to make room for the essentials? List three ways you can do that in the coming weeks.

4. What is the root of your yes? Write down the areas where you struggle to say no, and then write down the underlying thoughts and beliefs that might be contributing to each one.

FINISH HERE

DONE BUT NOT COMPLETE

You made it. You've stayed with me throughout this entire journey, lesson by lesson, page by page. And honestly, in and of itself that's a *huge* feat. A quick glance at my own bookshelf and I see piles of books that have been started but not completed. It says a lot that you got through 31 lessons. And I'm so proud of you—really, truly, a heart-gushing kind of proud.

And because I'm so proud of you, I also want to remind you of something: You are done with this book, but you're not finished. This is really just the beginning—the beginning of a life lived well. I don't say that to discourage you; I say that to empower you. I want to set you up for success and remind you that the road of change, healing, and growth is a process, not a once-and-done thing. It's not something you get from one book, one counseling session, one lesson, one decision, one practice, or one habit. It's something you have to consistently come back to—something you have to regularly choose to engage in.

You may have started this book with a certain goal in mind: a pattern you wanted to change, a habit you wanted to break, an area in your life you wanted to heal. And maybe as you're wrapping up this book you've found that things have started to shift. Mindsets are changing, emotions are making more sense, behaviors are shifting and evolving.

New areas have surfaced in need of attention. That's exciting, and something you should celebrate and be proud of. But remember, it's only the beginning. And that's really good news—because if this is only the beginning, that means it only gets better. There's more healing, growth, and change around the corner if you'll keep leaning into it.

CHANGE IS A PROCESS

I often talk about the stages of change, reminding my clients that there's a cycle to change rather than a one-size-fits-all approach. We talked about some of the stages of change throughout the pages of this book, but let me list them out for you in order with detail:

Stage 1: Precontemplation

The first stage of change is when something worth changing is finally on your radar. Maybe you go to the doctor and they're concerned with your BMI or blood pressure. Or maybe you finished a book or an article or a podcast about becoming healthy, and you're starting to wonder if there's something you need to work on. Maybe you were close to losing something or someone you love, and that near miss has you thinking. Either way, the first stage of change is precontemplation, meaning you haven't thought too much about change, but now it's at least on your radar. You aren't serious about change at this point, but something has caused you to at least consider that there may be areas in your life that could benefit from a change.

Stage 2: Contemplation

The second stage of change is when you finally start thinking through what it would look like to do things differently. You weigh the pros and cons of changing, and the scale starts tipping in the direction of change. At this point, maybe you're sick and tired of dealing with anxiety on a regular basis, and you've finally decided it's time to try to get help. Maybe you get on the scale and it's so far from your ideal healthy weight that you decide its finally time to do something about it. At this point in the stages of change, the motivation is beginning to grow. You see the problem more clearly than you ever have before. You've moved from considering change to wanting change.

Stage 3: Preparation

This is the stage when the process of change practically begins. You go from wanting something to getting ready for it. This would be the stage where you map out a plan of how you are going to get from point A to point B. If you're trying to lose weight, for example, you'd start educating yourself about nutrition and exercise, research some weight-loss apps, or plan out your weekly menu of healthy meals. A lot of people skip this important stage. They get motivated, and they want to skip right to the action stage. But there is so much value in preparation! You can't go from sitting on the couch and decide the next day you want to run a marathon. You've got to plan, and prepare, and train. This is what the preparation stage is all about. If you want to change something, you've got to have a plan.

Stage 4: Action

This is the stage most people think about when it comes to change, because it's the stage where you can actually see change happen. You start hitting the gym, or showing up to your counseling sessions, or attending that AA meeting, or get some accountability in your life. You start intentionally doing things differently instead of defaulting to what you've always done.

Remember how we talked about the fact that healing is not linear? Well, this is when you'll really see that come into play. Sometimes you'll be in the action phase for a while and then find yourself back in preparation mode, or even all the way back in contemplation, or precontemplation. Maybe you failed at something, or relapsed, or struggled again—and now you've got to get motivation back, tweak your plan, get better support, get back up and try again. Because eventually, as long as you don't give up, the action stage will lead you to the next stage of healing.

Stage 5: Maintenance

The last stage of healing is what it looks like to live changed, because eventually long-term actions lead to long-term habits. You've made progress and moved to a new place. You've worked through your trauma, found freedom from panic attacks, overcome your demons, said goodbye to that addiction, and reached the goals you were hoping to achieve. This doesn't mean you'll never struggle again, and in fact, maybe you'll always walk with a little bit of a limp in these areas. But you'll continue to push through, fight back, to get back up when you've been knocked down, because if you've done it once, you can do it again.

WHAT IS IT FOR YOU?

I have to wonder what it is that caused you to pick this book up in the first place. What is it in your life that needed a reset? I can only guess the thing you wanted to focus on, change, grow, shift, or heal. Maybe there was something really specific in your mind as you started this book, or maybe something vague. Maybe God began to highlight an area of your life as you read and revealed something that needed healing that you hadn't seen before. Whatever it is, I'm so proud of you that you've made it this far, that you've chosen to put in the work, that you've allowed yourself to learn, be challenged, and face the hard stuff.

I don't know where you are on the journey of healing right now, but I do know this: The fact that you're on the journey is a win. One step at a time, one practice at a time, one insight at a time, one habit at a time. With God's help, you're choosing to move yourself to a better place. And I'm so honored and grateful that you've trusted me with this part of your journey.

I want you to know that even though this book is finished, our time together isn't over. I want this book, these words, this message to be something you come back to practice. Something you pick up again and again in different seasons of your life as you tune into what's going on inside you and how it's affecting what's going on around you. I want these powerful habits to become so familiar that you often find yourself thinking about them in your routine, day-to-day life. I want them to be the set of tools you pick up and use regularly as you engage in the process of building change, constructing healing, and securing growth.

Maybe one day God will remind you to check in to own your thoughts, to question your emotions or shift your story. Maybe another day to pause, to rest, to practice soul-care and set healthy boundaries. Or perhaps you'll be challenged to go backward to go forward, to face the hard stuff, or to heal from childhood wounds.

Each day will look a little different and come with different challenges, needs, actions, and reactions. But if you keep these practices close to your heart, each day you will be equipped to handle what comes. Each day you'll be able to identify the thoughts that lead to the feelings that lead to the behaviors in your life. Each day you'll have another opportunity to practice caring for yourself and healing from the inside out.

PROGRESS, NOT PERFECTION

I want you to remember that life, the entirety of it, is a process. It's a cycle. It's a journey of healing one layer at a time. Just because you fail today doesn't mean you're going to fail tomorrow. Just because you mastered something today doesn't mean you won't need to practice again tomorrow. Again, healing is a journey; growth is a process; change isn't a once-and-done thing. When you see something come back in your life that you were hoping to get rid of once and for all, remember that healing happens in layers. This isn't a setback; it's just an opportunity for deeper healing—a new layer exposed and revealed is a new layer to be healed.

The goal isn't perfection; the goal is progress. The goal is that you keep moving and stay engaged. The goal is that 365 days from now, you're in a better place and have a healthier mindset, a stronger outlook, a deeper understanding of what's going on inside of you, and a clearer perspective of the way your thoughts lead to your feelings, which lead to your behaviors. The beautiful thing about our God is that He's never expected perfection from us, and He never will. In fact, He's already come up with the solution for our imperfection—and that solution is

Jesus. He sent Jesus to stand in the gap on our behalf, to offer His perfection so we can simply focus on the process (1 Peter 2:24). Instead of seeking perfection, we get to *engage* in the process. We get to *enjoy* the process. And the process is simply this: living this life as abundantly as we can.

My prayer for you as you journey through this beautiful process of growth, this cycle of change, these layers of healing again, and again, and again, is that you would feel more alive, more present, more healed, and freer—and that you would live life even more abundantly than ever before.

"Behold, I am making all things new," God tells us (Revelation 21:5 ESV). Did you hear that? He's doing something new. And this is only the beginning. Praise God, it's time for a reset!

IDENTIFYING AND TREATING MENTAL HEALTH STRUGGLES

Mental illness doesn't reflect a character issue; it reflects a chemistry issue. Mental illness is caused by changes in the functioning of neurochemicals in the brain (primarily serotonin and dopamine) that begin to affect the rest of the body. Just like we would prescribe insulin and lifestyle changes for a person with diabetes, we must also understand the role of proper medication and counseling for a person who is struggling with a mental health disorder. A mental health struggle is not a reflection of a person's strength or faith, and it's important to reiterate that to the struggling individual. There is hope for healing!

Depression and anxiety are two of the most commonly reported mental health struggles that are permeating the church at large. It's important to have a healthy understanding of how they present. Feeling "worry" is not the same as generalized anxiety. Feeling "sad" is not the same as major depressive disorder. It's not the feeling that defines the struggle; it's the presenting symptoms. If you have been feeling stuck for a significant amount of time, consider whether an undiagnosed and untreated mental health struggle may be holding you back. Here are a list of symptoms to consider. Please consult with a medical doctor or a licensed professional counselor if you exhibit the following symptoms.

MAJOR DEPRESSIVE DISORDER (MDD)

This is a common yet serious mood disorder that impacts a person's daily life. It's also referred to as clinical depression. This disorder is above and beyond the feeling of "sadness," and it permeates many parts of the individual's life. It can be diagnosed when a person exhibits five or more of the following symptoms in a two-week period:

- Depressed mood (most days, most of the day) including sadness, emptiness, hopelessness. Can also be perceived as crying more than usual.

- Loss of interest and pleasure. This can show up as a lack of excitement, joy, interest in relationships.

- Weight loss or gain and decrease or increase in appetite.

- Insomnia or hypersomnia (the inability to sleep well or sleeping too much).

- Psychomotor retardation or agitation (slowed movements).

- Fatigue or a lack of energy.

- Feelings of worthlessness or excessive guilt.

- Decreased concentration.

- Thoughts of suicide or death.

The above symptoms will negatively affect other areas of the person's life including work, social life, relationships, and more, and are not related to another medical condition or medication.

GENERALIZED ANXIETY DISORDER (GAD)

- The presence of excessive worry for a period of six months or more.

- The worry is experienced as very difficult to control and may move from one topic to another over time.

- The anxiety and worry are also accompanied by physical symptoms. (In adults, three of the following symptoms; in children only one, of the following is necessary for a diagnosis.)

  » Edginess or restlessness

  » Fatigue or consistent lack of energy

  » Difficulty concentrating

  » Irritability

  » Increased muscle aches or soreness

  » Difficulty sleeping (trouble falling asleep, staying asleep, restlessness at night or unsatisfying sleep)

The worry and anxiety displayed can revolve around a number of things, including health concerns for self or others, job responsibilities, financial concerns, or everyday life matters. It's often accompanied by a need to seek reassurance from others.

Generalized anxiety can be accompanied by panic attacks. Because panic attacks often present as physical symptoms, they can be hard to identify and often confused with a medical condition.

PANIC ATTACKS

- Chest pain or discomfort
- Shortness of breath
- Hot flashes or chills
- Excessive sweating
- Feeling of choking
- Fear of dying
- Fear of losing control or "going crazy"
- Feeling dizzy, faint, or lightheaded

- Accelerated heart rate or palpitations

- Nausea or abdominal stress

- Numbness or tingling sensations

- Feelings of unreality or being detached from oneself (called depersonalization)

- Trembling or shaking

Symptoms of a panic attack usually happen suddenly, last about ten minutes, and then subside. Some attacks may last longer or happen in succession. Panic disorder also causes the fear or worry that the episode may happen again. This sometimes causes the individual to avoid certain situations for fear of an episode.

HOW TO TREAT MENTAL ILLNESS

The following treatment methods are most effective in battling depression and anxiety.

Therapy

Therapy is a profound experience, unlike anything else, guiding you through the difficult emotions and hard experiences in a hope-filled way. It helps you counter faulty thinking, gives you skills to process difficult past experiences, and offers renewed perspective and hope for the future. And not only that, but it's proven to be effective as a primary treatment method for people struggling with mental illness. In fact, it can be just as effective as medication when it comes to treating mild to moderate mental illness.

There are online options now that make it more convenient than ever and offer an easier route for those who might be reluctant to go see a therapist in person. If you do not have a trusted therapist or need a guide to find a good therapist, visit www.DebraFileta.com/counseling for counseling resources and the opportunity to connect with me and my team at the Debra Fileta Counselors Network.

Medication

Medication is a recommended treatment method for people struggling with moderate to severe symptoms of anxiety and depression. The role of these medications (commonly known as antidepressants or SSRIs) is to increase the neurochemicals in the body that are responsible for regulating mood. Not only can they be beneficial to someone who is struggling, but they can be life changing. These medications can be prescribed by a medical doctor. If you've been feeling stuck for a significant amount of time, I challenge you to get a clinical assessment with a medical doctor or licensed counselor to rule out any underlying mental health struggles.

HOW TO FIND A COUNSELOR

Finding a good counselor can seem like a daunting process for many people. In fact, "How do I find a counselor?" is one of the most common questions I receive. To help you with this process, I put together this brief check list to get you started.

1. The most common route to finding a counselor (or pretty much anything these days) is by doing an internet search.

You want to make sure you are searching for a Licensed Counselor, and ideally, one who is also a Christian. There are many people who use the term "counselor" that may be pastorally certified, but not licensed by the state. The term *licensed* is really what you're looking for, as they are trained professionals who have undergone a specific amount of training and education.

2. Usually, a counselor's biography will list some of their areas of specialty such as sex therapy, trauma, depression and anxiety, addictions, and so forth.

Try to connect with a counselor who serves your specific area of struggle. Feel free to give them a call or send an email before scheduling your first session, asking them what type of therapy they typically use and how many years they've been in practice, as well as how they integrate the Christian faith into their clinical approach.

3. Remember that when it comes to finding a good counselor, it's all about finding someone you feel comfortable with.

The therapeutic relationship between you and your counselor is important, but it's not uncommon not to "hit it off" right away. I always recommend trying three to six sessions with a counselor before you attempt to find another one. If, after a handful of sessions, you don't feel the connection or don't feel comfortable, by all means don't quit counseling! Find another counselor and try again. There's no offense taken if you don't connect. The only true offense is if you give up on your situation! Reach out to another counselor (and in some cases even another *and another*) and try again.

4. Always remember that healing is not linear; it's cyclical.

Again, you don't just get better and better each day. Sometimes you'll take a few steps forward and one step back. Sometimes you'll struggle. Sometimes you'll want to give up. But the key is to continue moving forward, because as you do, you're getting healthier and stronger and closer to your goals. Healing is not only possible, but also *attainable* for those who are willing to put in the work.

5. Visit www.DebraFileta.com/counseling.

Visit my website for a list of resources as well as the option of connecting with me and my team at the Debra Fileta Counselors Network.

NOTES

START HERE

1. While I'm not referring to literal brain chemistry in this illustration, I do want to make it very clear that sometimes brain chemistry actually gets in the way of our healing, change, and growth. Mental illnesses, such as clinical depression or clinical anxiety actually change our brain chemistry and impede our physical and psychological motivations and abilities. Please see Appendix A for a list of symptoms of clinical anxiety and clinical depression as well as next steps.

CHAPTER 1—STOP BEFORE YOU START

1. Cara Bradley, "The Power of Pause," Mindful, August 15, 2018, www.mindful.org/the-power-of -pause.

2. Mary Helen Immordino-Yang, Joanna A. Christodoulou, and Vanessa Singh, "Rest Is Not Idleness: Implications of the Brain's Default Mode for Human Development and Education," *Perspectives on Psychological Science* 7, no. 4 (June 29, 2012): 352-64, doi:10.1177/1745691612447308.

3. Biblehub, s.v. "harpu," accessed April 11, 2022, www.https://biblehub.com/hebrew/harpu_7503 .htm.

CHAPTER 2—SOMETHING NEW

1. *True Love Dates* (for singles), *Love in Every Season* (for dating or engaged couples), and *Choosing Marriage* and *Married Sex* (for engaged or married couples).

2. If you find yourself feeling stuck in your relationship with God, hurt by Him, unable to deeply believe or expect, I want to point you to chapter 4 of my book *Are You Really OK?* (Eugene, OR: Harvest House Publishers, 2021). Here, we go for a deeper dive into ways the pain of our past influences the way we see God, and how to begin the process of healing.

CHAPTER 3—OWN YOUR JUNK

1. Mark D. Alicke and Olesya Govorun, "The Better-than-Average Effect," *The Self in Social Judgment* (New York: Psychology Press, 2005), 83-106.

CHAPTER 7—IT'S NOT A ONE-PLAYER GAME

1. Heidi Grant, "How to Get the Help You Need," Harvard Business Review, May–June 2018, www
.hbr.org/2018/05/how-to-get-the-help-you-need.

2. Heidi Grant, quoted in Angela Chen, "A Social Psychologist Explains Why We Should Ask
for Help More Often," The Verge, June 22, 2018, www.theverge.com/2018/6/22/17475134/
heidi-grant-reinforcements-help-social-psychology.

3. Chen, "A Social Psychologist Explains," The Verge.

CHAPTER 8—DEFAULT MODE

1. This is such an integral part of understanding mental and emotional health that an entire method
of therapy is committed to helping you understand the process. Cognitive Behavioral Therapy, or
CBT, was developed by Aaron T. Beck in the 1960s.

2. The ABC Model was developed by Dr. Albert Ellis in the 1950s.

CHAPTER 11—CALL OUT THE LIES

1. For more detailed examples, see chapter 7 of my book, *Are You Really OK?* (Eugene, OR: Harvest
House Publishers, 2021).

CHAPTER 14—LIKE A CHILD

1. R. Kent Hughes, "What Jesus Thinks About Children," Crossway, March 12, 2015, www.cross
way.org/articles/what-jesus-thinks-about-children.

CHAPTER 16—PRESSURE CHECK

1. What many people refer to as a mental breakdown usually falls into the category of a mental health
disorder. See Appendix A to read the signs and symptoms of clinical anxiety and clinical depression.

2. T. H. Holmes and R. H. Rahe, "The Social Readjustment Rating Scale," *Journal of Psychosomatic
Research* 11, no. 2 (August 1967): 213-18, doi:10.1016/0022-3999(67)90010-4.

3. "Anxiety Overload: On-Air Counseling Session with JP Pokluda," *Love and Relationships Podcast
with Debra Fileta*, March 15, 2022, www.truelovedates.com/are-you-really-ok-jp-pokluda-2.

CHAPTER 17—PRESSURE RELEASE

1. "Can Your Water Heater Explode? Warning Signs & Prevention," American Home Water & Air,
accessed April 20, 2022, www.americanhomewater.com/can-your-water-heater-explode.

2. For a good book on mindfulness, pick up Charles Stone's *Holy Noticing: The Bible, Your Brain, and
the Mindful Space Between Moments* (Chicago: Moody Publishers, 2019).

CHAPTER 18— FEEL FREE TO FEEL

1. "Afraid to Feel: On-Air Counseling with Mike Todd," *Love and Relationships Podcast with Debra
Fileta*, June 22, 2022, https://truelovedates.com/afraid-to-feel-on-air-counseling-with-mike-todd/.

2. Bill Gaultier, "How to Feel Your Emotions with Jesus," SoulShepherding.org, accessed February
16, 2022, www.soulshepherding.org/how-to-feel-your-emotions-with-jesus.

CHAPTER 19—NECESSARY INTERRUPTIONS

1. "Saving a Family from Carbon Monoxide Poisoning—Vivint Customer Story," YouTube, posted by Vivint, October 13, 2015, www.youtube.com/watch?v=giJ50f7Lmds.

CHAPTER 22—FEELINGS IN MY BODY

1. Asmir Gračanin, Lauren M. Bylsma, and Ad J.J.M. Vingerhoets, "Is Crying a Self-Soothing Behavior?" *Frontiers in Psychology* 5 (May 28, 2014): doi:10.3389/fpsyg.2014.00502.

2. Ed Diener and Micaela Y. Chan, "Happy People Live Longer: Subjective Well-Being Contributes to Health and Longevity," *Applied Psychology: Health and Well-Being* 3, no. 1 (March 2011), 1-43, doi:10.1111/j.1758-0854.2010.01045.x.

3. Habib Yaribeygi et al., "The Impact of Stress on Body Function: A Review," *EXCLI Journal* 16 (July 21, 2017): 1057-1072, doi:10.17179/excli2017-480.

4. Lauri Nummenmaa, Enrico Glerean, Riitta Hari, and Jari K. Hietanen, "Bodily Map of Emotions," *Proceedings of the National Academy of Sciences* 111, no. 2 (January 2014): 646-651, doi:10.1073/pnas.1321664111.

CHAPTER 23—WORK IT OUT

1. Debra L. Blackwell and Tainya C. Clarke, "State Variation in Meeting the 2008 Federal Guidelines for Both Aerobic and Muscle-strengthening Activities Through Leisure-time Physical Activity Among Adults Aged 18–64: United States, 2010–2015," *National Health Statistics Reports 112*, June 28, 2018, www.cdc.gov/nchs/data/nhsr/nhsr112.pdf.

2. Elizabeth Anderson and Geetha Shivakumar, "Effects of Exercise and Physical Activity on Anxiety," *Frontiers in Psychiatry* 4 (2013): doi:10.3389/fpsyt.2013.00027.

3. Ulrike Rimmele et al., "Trained Men Show Lower Cortisol, Heart Rate and Psychological Responses to Psychosocial Stress Compared with Untrained Men," *Psychoneuroendocrinology* 32, no. 6 (July 2007): 627-635, doi:10.1016/j.psyneuen.2007.04.005.

4. Anderson and Shivakumar, "Effects of Exercise and Physical Activity on Anxiety."

5. James Blumenthal et al., "Is Exercise a Viable Treatment for Depression?" *ACSM's Health & Fitness Journal* 16, no. 4 (July/August 2012): 14-21, doi:10.1249/01.FIT.0000416000.09526.eb.

6. K. Kamenov et al., "The Efficacy of Psychotherapy, Pharmacotherapy and Their Combination on Functioning and Quality of Life in Depression: A Meta-Analysis," *Psychological Medicine* 47, no. 3 (2017): 414-425, doi:10.1017/S0033291716002774.

CHAPTER 25—HEALTHY WITHDRAWAL

1. Brian A. Primack et al., "Social Media Use and Perceived Social Isolation Among Young Adults in the U.S.," *American Journal of Preventative Medicine* 53, no. 1 (July 1, 2017): 1-8, doi:10.1016/j.amepre.2017.01.010.

2. Christopher R. Long and James R. Averill, "Solitude: An Exploration of Benefits of Being Alone," *Journal for the Theory of Social Behaviour* 33, no. 1 (March 5, 2003): 21-44, doi:10.1111/1468-5914.00204.

3. Brent Crane, "The Virtues of Isolation," The Atlantic, March 30, 2017, www.theatlantic.com/health/archive/2017/03/the-virtues-of-isolation/521100.

CHAPTER 26—THE 8:8:8 RULE

1. Anna McEvinney, "Why Do We Have an 8-Hour Working Day?" History Guild, November 6, 2020, www.historyguild.org/why-do-we-have-an-8-hour-working-day.

2. See chapter 10 of my book *Are You Really OK?* for more on sleep hygiene (Eugene, OR: Harvest House Publishers, 2022).

CHAPTER 27—INHALE AND EXHALE

1. Caragh Behan, "The Benefits of Meditation and Mindfulness Practices During Times of Crisis Such as COVID-19," *Irish Journal of Psychological Medicine* 37, no. 4 (December 2020): 256-258, doi:10.1017/ipm.2020.38

2. Charles Stone, *Holy Noticing: The Bible, Your Brain, and the Mindful Space Between Moments* (Chicago: Moody Publishers, 2019), 81-96.

3. Stone, *Holy Noticing*, 81-96.

4. Stone, *Holy Noticing*, 81-96.

CHAPTER 28—KNOW YOUR ENEMIES

1. Levi Lusko, in the foreword to Debra Fileta, *Are You Really OK?* (Eugene, OR: Harvest House Publishers, 2022), 10.

2. American Academy of Sleep Medicine. "Sleep Deprivation Affects Moral Judgment, Study Finds." ScienceDaily. www.sciencedaily.com/releases/2007/03/070301081831.htm (accessed August 26, 2022).

CHAPTER 29—STAY ATTACHED

1. R. Chris Fraley and Michael J. Marks, "Westermarck, Freud, and the Incest Taboo: Does Familial Resemblance Activate Sexual Attraction?" *Personality and Social Psychology Bulletin* 36, no. 9 (September 2010): 1202-12, doi:10.1177/0146167210377180.

2. Krispin Mayfield, *Attached to God: A Practical Guide to Deeper Spiritual Experience* (Grand Rapids, MI: Zondervan, 2022).

3. Mayfield, *Attached to God.*

CHAPTER 30—DISTRACTIONS ALL AROUND

1. Harriet Griffey, "The Lost Art of Concentration: Being Distracted in a Digital World," *Guardian*, October 14, 2018, www.theguardian.com/lifeandstyle/2018/oct/14/the-lost-art-of-concentration-being-distracted-in-a-digital-world.

2. Ofcom, "UK Communications Market Report," August 2, 2018, www.ofcom.org.uk/__data/assets/pdf_file/0022/117256/CMR-2018-narrative-report.pdf.

CHAPTER 31—CONCENTRATE AND ELIMINATE

1. Anne Ortlund, *Disciplines of the Beautiful Woman* (Nashville, TN: W Publishing Group, 1984), 48.

2. For a really great sermon on focus, prioritizing, and busyness, check out Pastor JP Pokluda's sermon "Busyness: 7 Deadly Sins of Suburbia" on YouTube, posted by Harris Creek Baptist Church, January 9, 2022, www.youtube.com/watch?v=H1VvwkzILfo.

ABOUT THE AUTHOR

Debra Fileta, M.A., LPC is a licensed professional counselor, national speaker, and the founder of the Debra Fileta Counselors Network. She's the author of *Are You Really OK?*, *Choosing Marriage, Love in Every Season, True Love Dates,* and *Married Sex.* Through her popular blog (TrueLoveDates.com) and podcast (*Love and Relationships*), she shares the message that healthy people make healthy relationships. Debra and her husband, John, have been happily married for 15 years and have four beautiful children.

www.TrueLoveDates.com

www.DebraFileta.com

ARE YOU REALLY OK?

Pursuing the spiritual, emotional, mental, and physical health God desires for you is a lifelong commitment that requires honest self-examination and intentional living. In *Are You Really OK?* author and licensed counselor Debra Fileta will help you take inventory of yourself so you can recognize where you need growth and healing.